RESEARCH AIRCRAFT 1891–19?

X-PLANES

A UNIQUE PICTORIAL RECORD
OF FLYING PROTOTYPES, THEIR DESIGNERS AND PILOTS

RESEARCH AIRCRAFT 1891–1970

X-PLANES

A UNIQUE PICTORIAL RECORD
OF FLYING PROTOTYPES, THEIR DESIGNERS AND PILOTS

HUGH W. COWIN

First published in Great Britain in 1999 by Osprey Publishing,
Elms Court, Chapel Way, Botley, Oxford OX2 9LP
Email: osprey@osprey-publishing.co.uk

ISBN 1 85532 876 3

Managing Editor: Shaun Barrington
Editor: Marcus Cowper
Design: the Black Spot
Origination by Microset Imaging, Witney, United Kingdom
Printed through World Print Limited, Hong Kong

99 00 01 02 03   10 9 8 7 6 5 4 3 2 1

Other titles from Osprey Aviation include:

Boeing Aircraft Cutaways, Mike Badrocke & Bill Gunston
ISBN 185532 785 6

Combat Aircraft 10: *SBD Dauntless Units of WWII*, Barrett Tillman
ISBN 185532 732 5

Aircraft of the Aces 22: *Japanese Navy Aces 1937-45*, Henry Sekaida
ISBN 185532 727 9

Airbus Jetliners, Robbie Shaw
ISBN 185532 868 2

Future titles in Osprey's Aviation Pioneers series include:

AP2: *The Risk Takers: Racing & Record-breaking Aircraft*,
publication September 1999.

AP3 and 4: *World War I Aircraft* and *Black Jet: - US Stealth Aircraft*,
publication 2000.

For a catalogue of all books published by Osprey Military,
Automotive and Aviation, please write to:
**The Marketing Manager, Osprey Publishing, PO Box 140,
Wellingborough, Northants, NN8 4ZA, United Kingdom**

Visit Osprey's website at:
http://www.osprey-publishing.co.uk

Acknowledgements
I am lastingly grateful to Ray Funnel, M. J. 'Mike' Hooks,
Hans Justus Meier and E. 'Teddy' Nevill of TRH Pictures,
all of whom provided a great deal of support in one form
or another. I must also thank Andrew Siddons of Rolls-Royce
and Keith Mordoff of Lockheed Martin for their rapid
response in providing last minute help. I am also indebted
to the countless industry and operator publicists whose
photographic press releases have, over the past forty or
more years, provided many of the picture sources quoted
in brackets at the end of the caption.

Front cover, above The Edwards Rhomboidal Biplane, 1911;
see page 14.

Front cover, below The Douglas X-3, 1952; see page 77.
(Douglas)

Front cover, right Wing Commander Roland Beamont (left),
before the maiden flight of the TSR-2. (British Aerospace)

Back cover The Northrop Avion Flying Wing, 1929;
see page 34.

Contents

Title page With its 131 feet 3 inch wingspan and an all-up-weight of 44,672lb, design of the six 450hp Napier Lion-powered **Tarrant Tabor** began in the latter stages of World War I. It was intended to carry a 1,500lb bombload to Berlin from an English airfield. Estimated to have had a top level speed of 110mph, F 1765, the sole example of the Tabor built, was readied for its maiden flight from the Royal Aircraft Establishment at Farnborough on 26 May, 1919. The pilot and co-pilot selected to make the flight were Captains F.G. Dunn and P.T. Rawlings. For whatever reason, it was decided that the first take-off run would be attempted with only the lower four engines at full throttle. However, as the colossal machine rolled across the airfield, the pilots brought both of the upper engines to full power, causing the aircraft to nose over into the ground and to inflict fatal injuries on both men. (RAE, Crown Copyright)

The sole **Boulton Paul P.120** had one of the shortest flying careers of all, even for a research aircraft (see page 65). The second of two Boulton Paul P.111 research machines, VT951 became the P.120 when it was decided to equip the aircraft with a revised fin and rudder to which a 'slab', or all-flying tailplane was attached. (Boulton Paul)

Preface

Back in the 1950s a friend presented me with a framed print of a Curtiss JN lodged in a treetop, clearly having come out the loser from the impact. Below the image was the printed observation that aviation was not inherently dangerous, but was extremely unforgiving of the foolish. Having spent the intervening years within aviation, I would argue that while the first part of the statement might apply to airline passengers, it is just not so for those working in aircraft development. With regard to the second assertion, I can only heartily concur.

As the most superficial glance through will show, this book tends to concentrate on aviation's calamities, rather than its triumphs. For this I make no apology. The reason for focusing on aviation's tribulations is straightforward. Unlike the triumphs, a great amount of behind-the-scenes effort is often expended to draw a veil over a mishap. Thus, a disaster tends, with time, to be forgotten, a pity in itself, as in many cases, the details of the setback could well have served as pointers on how not to do it; and the disasters sometimes reveal more about the direction of development thinking at any point in history than the successes.

When I set off to write this book the intention was to bring it right up to date with references to the latest in research, such as the unmanned X-33 aerospace project and the X-38 re-entry lifeboat. The Publisher, mindful of page constraints, urged me to choose an earlier cut-off point. The more I thought about this, the more sense it made to cut off at 1970. Aviation developments have little direct link with the calendar, they are paced by the amount of money and, hence, effort expended. Looking back over the period since 1970 appears to show that, while not stopping, aviation developments have been much fewer than could have been justifiably anticipated. With the exception of a handful of Concordes, airliner speeds are little different from that of the Boeing 707 of 1958, while, in the military arena, the only real development has been stealth technology. Based on the limited numbers of Lockheed F-117s and Northrop B-2s that even the US can afford, stealth will be out of reach for the majority of would-be users for a long time to come. The first production combat fighter capable of emulating the 1964 Lockheed SR-71's sustained supersonic cruise, Lockheed Martin's F-22 Raptor, will not enter service until after the Millennium.

The structure of this book is of course chronological, with certain fundamental concepts presented in separate chapters. Interspersed within the entries for aircraft are brief biographies of some of the prime movers and shakers of aircraft history.

Finally, for those perturbed to find nothing other than imperial measure being used throughout this book, I must simply point to the fact that within current international aviation practice, imperial measure is the standard. 'Metrication advances, casting its penumbra upon us all. Once we are in its grasp, Europe, the Common Market and ELDO/ESRO will see us an equal. Those of us, that is, who survive the ordeal.'(Aerospace Review, November 1970.)

Early Essays, 1891–1912

T he German, Otto Lilienthal, had made his first heavier-than-air flight in 1891, some twelve years ahead of the Wright Brothers historic powered hop of 17 December 1903. By 1894, Lilienthal's progress was such that his No.11 design was gliding over distances of up to 1,150 feet, or nearly ten times the length of the Wright Brothers' first powered flight. By 1896, others had joined Lilienthal in making heavier-than-air flights, prominent among which were Lawrence Hargraves' box kite ascents of 1894, Percy Picher's Lilienthal-influenced Bat glider of 1895 and the Octave Chanute biplane glider of 1896 flown by A. M. Herring. Incidentally, all four of these designers were contemplating powering their craft.

The differences between all of the precursors to the Wright Brothers and their 1903 Flyer not only lay in the lack of power: they were all inherently stable craft, capable, essentially, of only flying straight ahead. Surprisingly, even after the Wright Brothers had placed emphasis on the need to introduce an element of manoeuvrability through the use of co-ordinated rudder and wing warping, this all-important aspect of aircraft control was totally overlooked for more than five years. Between 1902 and 1907, all of the Wright Brothers' peers directed their efforts towards achieving inherent stability. Ironically Lilienthal's death resulted directly from his designs' lack of roll/lateral control.

Only very slowly did the notion of wing warping, or some other form of roll control appear to sink in, emerging in France initially with Henry Farman at the end of 1907 and in the US the following June, with the Glenn Curtiss-designed June Bug. Both spurned the Wright wing warping system in favour of ailerons.

The evolution of the aero-engine was the other pressing matter and, until the arrival of the first relatively high-powered, lightweight Gnome rotary in mid-1908, flying machines had depended almost completely on adaptations of existing low power-to-weight car or motorcycle engines. Soon, the majority of aircraft constructors were using rotaries, as they would until well into World War I.

Thus, by 1909 the emergence of adequate power was pushing aircraft speed and altitude performance rapidly upwards.

By 1912, the shape of the flying machine had been basically settled. The French, who at this time led the world, predominantly favoured the tractor, or front-mounted, pulling-engine monoplane, while the US remained more conservatively fixed on the pusher, or rear-mounted engine biplane. Britain, running way behind the leading nations, produced mediocre aircraft of both layouts. The canard, or back-to-front layout with the tail ahead of the mainplane so favoured by the first wave of constructors, had virtually vanished by the end of this period, subsequently reappearing only occasionally over the years until relatively recently, when, with the emergence of advanced flight control systems, it has once more found favour with front-line combat aircraft designers.

Previous page A fascinating 1904 or 1905 view of **Robert Esnault-Pelterie** road testing a new wing section. Note the rearward facing 'flight test observer'. This approach was typical of that adopted by the Europeans at this time, who, unlike the Wright Brothers, tested items piecemeal, rather than integrating everything into flyable form and evolving the machine based on practical experience. If a European's design failed at the first attempt, the practice appears to have been not to tinker with it, but to go back to square one. (Cowin Collection)

Otto Lilienthal flying his **No. 13** design, the first of two biplane gliders he built in 1895. He was to be fatally injured on 9 August 1896, while gliding his standard and much-flown No.11 monoplane design. (US National Archives)

Although this **Phillips Multiplane** of 1904 was the third of the heavier-than-air designs by the English scientist, Horatio F. Phillips, it was also the first of his machines aimed at free flight. Sadly, the wing structure proved inadequate for the lift produced

and the whole array folded upwards on its first attempt to fly. The two designs Phillips had produced previously were actually more successful than the 1904 Multiplane, both having 'lifted-off' successfully during the 1893-1894 period. These earlier machines were never intended for free flight, being more in the nature of aerodynamic lift demonstrators, operating off a circular track around a centre post from which they were tethered. In the course of these experiments, the second of these lift demonstrators briefly carried an all-up-weight of 385lb aloft. A scientist, rather than an engineer, Horatio Phillips (b. 1845) made such a significant contribution to the understanding of airfoil, or wing section shaping, that many consider him the true father of modern aerodynamics. (US National Archives)

Alberto Santos-Dumont was born into the family of an extremely rich Brazilian coffee planter in 1873. Learning his mechanical skill working on the locomotives his father used around the plantation, Santos-Dumont's infatuation with things that fly was triggered by the sight of ballooning during a family visit to Paris in 1891. Six years later and now Paris-based, he made his first balloon ascent, an event that was to set him, once and for all, on a career in aeronautics. In 1901, Santos-Dumont, who designed and flew his own balloons and airships, piloted his No. 6 dirigible around the Eiffel Tower from his base in nearby St. Cloud to win a FF 100,000 prize and the acclaim of all France. Turning to heavier-than-air flying in 1906, Santos-Dumont had the Voisin Brothers build him a box kite type design of canard, or back-to-front layout, his No.14 which was first flown suspended from beneath one of his dirigibles. Initially powered by 24hp Antoinette and now detached from the airship as the No. 14bis, this machine commenced flying in September 1906, but never succeeded in rising higher than two feet or so from the ground. Re-engined with a 50hp Antoinette, the No. 14bis then started out making a series of progressively improving hops in October and early November, culminating with Santos-Dumont's flights of 12 November 1906, that brought him official recognition as the first man to make a heavier-than-air flight in Europe. Around the close of 1909, Santos-Dumont contracted multiple sclerosis, whose onset forced the former intrepid aviator to retire from active flying and to return home to Brazil. No doubt more and more frustrated by his condition and the use of his beloved flying machines for military purposes that he so despised, this once famous flyer took his own life in 1932. (US National Archives)

Santos-Dumont flying his **No.14bis** over the Bagatelle meadows on the then outskirts of Paris. Note the wicker basket in which he stands, strange to modern eyes, but not so for a man brought up with balloons as he had been. First flown with a 24hp Antoinette engine on 13 September 1906, following tethered testing, the No. 14bis proved underpowered and was given a 50hp engine of the same make. So equipped, the No. 14bis made a much better job of things, reaching a height of 10

feet and covering a distance of 195 feet on October 23rd. However, this was a mere prelude to his officially observed six flights of November 12th, 1906, when with a height of around 20 feet and a distance of 720 feet, Santos-Dumont earned the title of being the first man to make a heavier-than-air flight in Europe. Worthy of comment is the fact that like all other European designs of the time, the No. 14bis was incapable of turning and as a box kite represented a totally sterile development path, as Henry Farman would shortly prove. (U.S .National Archives)

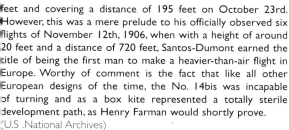

Above right The 1907 **Voisin Biplane** was the most successful of France's first wave of powered machines. The example seen here was sold to Englishman J. T. C. Moore-Brabazon, who was to become holder of the first British pilot's licence. This machine employs the 'curtained' interplane struts derived from the Voisin Brothers' earlier box kite-style glider floatplanes of 1904. Incidentally, Henry Farman had bought a 1907 Voisin and had expected to buy this particular machine, too. Farman, feeling betrayed by Gabrielle Voisin, decided he could do better and he did.

Below Wilbur Wright, seen here at the controls of the early 1908 **Wright Model A** after he had brought it to France later that year. Having achieved so much by 1905, the patent-conscious Wright Brothers decided, at the close of their 1905 flying season, to do no more flying for the moment, while they attempted to exploit the commercial worth of their efforts. In these endeavours they were only partially successful, in selling their designs for others to build, but not stopping the work of people like Glenn H. Curtiss, who insisted that the Wrights held no exclusive rights to the design of the generic aeroplane itself. Thus, somewhat disillusioned and with aviation now gaining far more attention in Europe than in their homeland, the Wrights decided to modify their prone-seated 1905 Flyer III into the Model A, with its 30hp Wright-designed engine and two, side-by-side upright seats, setting sail for a series of demonstration flights in France, the heartland of European aviation. Based in the Le Mans area between August and the end of 1908, Wilbur flew 104 times during this period, taking the French by storm, his last flight of 31 December being of 2 hours 20 minutes duration and covering around 77 miles. Incidentally, the Model A, like the Flyer II and III before it, was

actually catapult-launched into the air with the assistance of a weight and pulley system, in which a weight was released to fall from a small mast and whose momentum was transferred via the launching track to accelerate the machine's take-off. The one design feature that the Wright Brothers appear to have picked up from the Europeans is the use of wheels, absent from their Model A, but subsequently adopted on their 1910 Model B, which, notably, still clung to wing warping rather than ailerons for roll control. (US National Archives)

___

Top left **Robert Esnault-Pelterie's REP.2,** the French engineer's second powered flying machine, flew in 1908 and proved more successful than the REP.1, first flown in November 1907. Both were monoplanes, a configuration that the REPs must be credited with popularising. An interesting feature of the REPs were their use of wing warping, particularly as Esnault-Pelterie had invented and fitted the aileron, or more accurately in this particular case the elevon, as an alternative to wing warping for his modified Wright Glider of October 1904 – and he had vilified the idea of wing warping in his 1905 papers. (*Cowin Collection*)

Below The **Santos-Dumont No. 19,** first flown in November 1907, powered by a 20hp Dutheil-Chalmers engine, only managed three hops, the longest of which covered 656 feet. After being damaged on the 21st of the same month it was put in 'mothballs' until the close of the following year. The No. 19 had followed a barren period for Santos-Dumont, who, after the success of his No. 14bis, produced a series of unsuccessful designs. The No.19 must have come near to totally dispiriting its designer, who was aiming a producing a light aircraft for leisure use. Re-emerging in late 1908 as the No. 19bis, the re-worked machine this time stubbornly refused to leave the ground. With gritted teeth, the expatriate Brazilian set about a further re-build, this time re-numbered as the No. 20 of March 1909. Vindicated at last by the success of his No. 20 Demoiselle, Santos-Dumont is generally considered to be the father of the high wing light-plane tourers of the late 1920s onwards. (US National Archives)

___

Above The first of Henry Farman's own designs, the **Henry Farman III,** with its 50hp Vivinus engine, made its maiden flight

during April 1909, and soon consolidated Farman among the front rank of French aviators. For the record, Henry Farman's No. I had been a 1907 Voisin as mentioned above, his No II was the same machine, which from late 1907 into 1908, he modified progressively, first removing the inter-wing curtains and then by embodying ailerons. It was with this machine that Farman set many records including that for making the first circular flight over a I kilometre, or 0.62-mile course at Issy near Paris on 13 January 1908. The success of his own first real design, which sold in some numbers, was to propel Henry and his brother, Maurice, into becoming aircraft manufacturers in their own right. The fact that Farman spelt his forename with a 'y', not an 'i' suffix is verified on the fins of all his aircraft of this period. (Cowin Collection)

Above Pictured here the **Maquis d' Equevilly-Monjustin's Multiplane**. Described as being ' Very resilient, very light, very solid and cheap.' this contraption appeared in 1908 and was powered by an 8hp 3-cylinder air-cooled engine. Clearly influenced by Horatio Phillips' earlier Multiplanes, the pilot 'flies' the device from a standing position, not just the 'draggiest', but also the chilliest way of doing things. Unsurprisingly, no evidence of this machine ever flying can be found, an undisguised blessing for any would-be pilot, whose life would have been put in jeopardy by the self-evident lack of inherent pitch axis, or fore-and-aft stability.

Hervé, not Henri, **Fabre**, according to authoritative French sources, seen here standing beside the pusher propeller of his second design, the Canard, in which he made his first flight ever

on 28 March 1910 and also the world's first successful flight of a powered seaplane. Fabre, on that occasion, flew from Martigues, near his home in Marseilles, but much of the Canard's subsequent flying was to be from Monaco. Born into a Marseilles shipping family in 1882, Fabre embarked upon his research into hydrodynamics and floats during 1907. By 1909, Fabre had completed his first aircraft, which resolutely refused to fly, a not uncommon occurence in those early days. Success and recognition came

with the Canard in March 1910. After re-building and modifying Canard, Fabre built a wheel-equipped biplane that made little impact on the world of aviation and, from 1911 onwards, he turned to producing floats for other aircraft manufacturers. (US National Archives)

Overleaf The **Fabre Canard** in flight and in its later form, just prior to its March 1911 mishap when, following a poorly judged landing by one of France's leading motor boat racers, it was damaged beyond economic repair. Ironically, the Canard had been severely damaged during the previous summer at the hands of another of France's prominent aviators. Fabre, it should be noted, who had nowhere near the flying experience

of either man, managed to avoid inflicting such damage on his machine. As can be seen from the picture, the pilot sits astride the upper of the two 'fuselage' booms and controlled the top foreplane elevator via a tiller-like arm that only appears to be directly attached to his head. The profile and inclination of the machine's three pontoon floats is also well illustrated in this view. (US National Archives)

The Voisin Brothers were among the first, along with Glenn Curtiss in the US, to follow Fabre's successful pioneering of waterborne powered flight. Here is one of several **Voisin Canard**, or tail-first biplane floatplanes produced during 1911. Voisin canards with both three and four pontoons were built. The three-pontoon type seen here had wheels added at a later

date. In this modified guise, the machine took off from Issy airfield, with the Voisins' partner, Maurice Colliex, at the controls, to land on the river Seine. This flight, made in August 1911 is the first recorded successful flight by a waterborne aircraft. Note the Voisins' adoption of the aileron in place of wing warping. (Cowin Collection)

Right Other than the knowledge that the **Edwards Rhomboidal Biplane** was produced in Britain during 1911, little on this particular machine appears to have survived the years. What can be said, however, is that even at a time when virtually every new design was truly experimental, the Edwards machine was certainly different. The first of two points of interest clearly visible in this photograph is the purely accidental selection by the designer of a modern, tricycle landing gear arrangement, in this case chosen simply to ensure that the machine did not tip over onto nose or tail when at rest on the ground. Secondly, the machine's method of power transmission, using chain drives with multiple right-angled power take-offs may have been similar to those used by the

Wrights' 1903 Flyer, but actually has its roots in the first mechanical power transmission systems used in the early industrial mills of more than a century before

---

Above Unlike the telephone, the **Bell Cygnet III** of 1912 was not one of Dr Alexander Graham Bell's more earth-shattering inventions. In fact, the Cygnet III represented the last in a whole series of tetrahedral-cell winged designs by the good Doctor that started inauspiciously and got worse from there on. Along with his wife and other such future luminaries as Glenn H. Curtiss and J. A. D. McCurdy, Alexander Graham Bell had been a founder of the Aerial Experiment Association, set up during early 1908 at Hammondsport, in upstate New York.

Apparently obsessed by the potential aerodynamic promise of the tetrahedral cell structure made up of four triangular surfaces, Bell's first design, the man-carrying unpowered kite Cygnet I employed this peculiar geometric form. Apparently just capable of flying, this was followed by the monolithic, perhaps more aptly pyramid-sized, Cygnet II of 1909, with its Curtiss-designed 50hp engine that proved quite inadequate to the task of powering the giant aloft. Finally, in 1912, came the Cygnet III, seen here with the noted early Canadian aviator J.A. D. McCurdy at the controls. The nearest Cygnet III came to flying was in March 1912, when it rose a foot or so off the ground under the power of its 70hp Gnome rotary, just prior to suffering its ultimate, barely in-flight structural failure. (US National Archives)

A frontal aspect on Prof. Heinrich Focke's 1936 twin rotored **Focke Achgelis FA 61**, which, although emerging later than the initially comparable Breguet-Dorand co-axial rotored Gyroplane Laboratoire helicopter of the previous year, soon overtook its French rival to gain recognition as the world's first truly practical helicopter. (VFW)

Helicopter Hopefuls, 1907-1957

The helicopter, as a practical proposition, took a long time in coming. Its technical evolution proved far more of a challenge than had been expected. It is debatable whether the first generation of designs, that is the two rival French machines of 1907, could ever have raised themselves aloft, were it not for their operating strictly within the zone of 'ground effect'. One drawback that Sir George Cayley foesaw and others, including Thomas Edison, later quantified, was that the helicopter would always require more total installed power to rise vertically from the ground than would be needed by a fixed winged aircraft carrying a comparable load. The necessary mechanical complexity of simply maintaining inherent stability from a rotating wing remained the major technical hurdle to surmount for the first twenty or more years of actual helicopter flight. Consider what the best helicopters had achieved at the end of 1934: in terms of distance the world record stood at 1,184 yards, the altitude record was 57 feet and helicopter forward speeds were hardly more than an average person could run. To compound matters the helicopter also faced a very serious rival in the shape of the autogiro, which in its earliest form may not have been capable of vertical ascent, but got close enough to meet most requirements. Ironically, while the autogiro can be seen as a rival in the commercial sense, the solutions it offered in achieving inherent dynamic stability were gladly snatched up by the helicopter designers, who collectively had not addressed the problem with anything like the clarity of the autogiro inventor, Juan de la Cierva.

The sheer indifference helicopters appeared to engender from those outside the dedicated, but very small, helicopter designing community, was marked. Unlike the fixed-winged aircraft, which was beginning to attract government money by 1911, the helicopter missed out altogether in terms of government development support, as the case of Frenchman Paul Cornu shows. Even in the most aviation-conscious country at that time, Cornu's development work ultimately ground to a halt when he ran out of cash. The helicopter really did not begin to look credible until after the emergence of the Focke Achgelis Fa 61, the appearance of which coincided with the Nazi Party's propaganda desire to extol the superiority of German technology. Thus, for the first time, a helicopter was the recipient of previously undreamed-of sums of government money and the world's first really attention-focusing vertical riser was developed. Looking across the Atlantic underlines the importance of government development funding. Igor Sikorsky spent three years in his own little 'technological wilderness', before US entry into World War II led to the first paltry orders for his R-4 helicopter from the US Army and Navy. Even after this point, it was still to take a succession of wars in Korea, Algeria and South East Asia to make the helicopter and its industry independent, no longer reliant on direct government financial support to survive.

Left The Frenchman, **Paul Cornu**, sitting in his 1907 helicopter. Powered by a 24hp Antoinette engine, this fore-and-aft, tandem motored machine lifted its designer/pilot to the height of 1 foot for 20 seconds on 13 November 1907 to establish the world's first free-flying helicopter lift-off. Cornu's French rival, the Gyroplane I devised by Louis Breguet and Prof. Charles Richet had successfully taken a man aloft some six or so weeks earlier, on 29 September. However, as the Gyroplane lacked stability, it required four men standing at four corners and armed with poles to push and prod it in order to prevent its toppling, thus eliminating it from consideration as a free flier. (US National Archives)

Above A revealing view of the 1907 **Cornu helicopter**, with its 24hp Antoinette engine and twin, tandem disposed belt driven twin-bladed rotors. The two surfaces at the fore-and-aft extremities of the machine are stabiliser planes. As with other designers of his time, Cornu, lacking modern-day systems and component supplier support, had to improvise by using such 'off-the-shelf' items as standard bicycle wheels. (US National Archives)

The **Breguet-Richet Gyroplane No. II** of early 1908 was a much grander specimen than the original man-lifting Gyroplane of the previous year. If the initial machine had been little more than a 'lift demonstrator', requiring external aid to save it from toppling, the Gyroplane No. II was a far more ambitious hybrid of half-aeroplane-half-helicopter. Seen here in its initial form, the Gyroplane No. II still employs the biplane-type rotors of its precursor. Powered by a 55hp Renault engine, the Gyroplane No. II proved grossly overweight and underpowered when tested in the spring of 1908 and, clearly, required fairly major, weight-stripping surgery. This completed, the No. IIbis as it was now known re-emerged with monoplane-type rotors and much less of its aeroplane structure. In this guise, the No. IIbis rose to a height of 13 feet on 22 July 1908, but still lacking any real stability, was severely damaged on landing. (US National Archives)

In general, World War I not only ignored the helicopter; it actually deprived it of development effort as its few proponents were diverted to do more useful things with fixed winged aircraft. However, in the wake of the Great War came a handy supply of powerful, yet cheap war-surplus engines and parts that could be put to good use. The Marquis de Pateras Pescara, Argentinian by birth but resident in France, was one who exploited the war-surplus opportunity. Having first become involved with helicopters in 1919, Pescara had built two helicopters of little significance, prior to his **Pescara No. 3** that

did draw attention. Fitted with a 180hp Hispano-Suiza, water-cooled engine, the machine weighed around a ton and first flew in 1923 at Issy, near Paris, where it is seen here. By January 1924, the Pescara No. 3, despite a pronounced lack of stability, particularly along its fore-and-aft axis, was capable of hovering at a height of around 3 feet and managed to remain airborne for 10 minutes, 10 seconds. The Pescara No. 3 was the first to incorporate a practical cyclic pitch control that aided stability by balancing rotor lift between advancing and retreating rotor blades. While the No. 3's engine certainly offered plenty of power, its weight, along with that of its Lamblin radiator – the barrel-like device at the machine's rear – must have contributed significantly to its one ton all-up weight. (US National Archives)

Right The **Cierva C-4**, brainchild of Spaniard, Juan De La Cierva and his first demonstrably successful autogiro. It was completed at the end of 1922 and a month later took the aviation world by storm with a 4 kilometre, or 4,375 yard closed-circuit flight officially timed at 3 minutes, 30 seconds, representing a speed of 42.6mph, when flown by Flying Officer Gomez Spencer at an airfield near Madrid, on 31 January 1923. This at a time when what few helicopters there were would be pressed to achieve 4mph. Cierva had come to rotary wing design in 1919 unencumbered by any helicopter preconceptions. What Cierva was seeking was to produce an unstallable aircraft, that is, one that would continue to fly rather than to drop out of the sky should it be flown too slowly. It just so happened that he chose to exploit the properties of an autorotating rotor system. By this means the autogiro can descend back to earth at angles of up to 80 degrees, but land gently within a space of a few dozen feet at most. Initially troubled by the same instability problems that were besetting the aspirant helicopter developers, Cierva's non-driven rotor troubles proved far easier and quicker to tame. Indeed, his pioneering of the flapping and dragging rotor arm hinges was to solve many of the helicopter's longest standing problems at a stroke.

First flown on 26 June 1936, the **Focke Achgelis Fa 61** remained aloft for a mere 28 seconds on that occasion. By January 1939, D-EBVU, along with its sister had changed the pace of the helicopter saga from one of stumbling, snail-like progress into one of real promise, holding the records for helicopter speed, 76.15mph; height, 11,240 feet and helicopter distance of 143.05

miles. Powered by a single 160hp Bramo Sh 14A, the tw[...] rotored Fa 61 was to be directly developed into the similar[...] configured, but larger Fa 226, the world's first productio[...] transport helicopter. Incidentally, the small propeller in th[...] aircraft's nose provided little or no forward impulsion and wa[...] there, basically, to cool the engine, particularly when th[...] machine was hovering with no natural airflow to cool it. (VFW[...]

Right The **Herrick Convertaplane HV-2A**, NX 13515, wa[...] first flown in the summer of 1937. In essence, the aim of i[...] creator, Gerald Herrick, was to produce a get-you-down-safe[...] machine that took off and climbed away in normal fashion wit[...] its upper, bi-convex section wing fixed and locked as seen her[...] In an emergency, however, this upper wing could be released t[...] rotate, turning this 125hp kinner-engined two seater into a[...] autogiro of sorts. Herrick's first 1931 attempt crashed durir[...] its initial attempt at in-flight conversion. This machine wa[...] slightly more successful, but, not surprisingly, lacked stability i[...] the autorotative mode, thanks to its lack of rotor head hingin[...]

Overleaf Born in Kiev, Russia on 25 May 1889, **Igor Ivanovitc[...] Sikorsky's** fascination with rotary winged craft surface[...] early, when at the age of twelve, he built and flew his ow[...]

model helicopter. In 1908 Sikorsky visited Paris, returning with an Anzani engine and the advice to stay away from direct-lifters. Oblivious to this wisdom, Sikorsky had built two helicopters by 1910, neither of which flew. At the same time, the young Russian had built his first two fixed wing machines, the latter of which had lifted its proud designer/pilot off the ground for the first time. Flushed by this success, Sikorsky abandoned thoughts of helicopters for the while and, by 1913, was producing the largest aeroplane extant, sire to the world's first heavy bombers. Emigrating to the US in 1917, Sikorsky was to spend some years of impoverishment before he, once again, started to build aeroplanes. It was not until the late 1930s that he was able to return to his first love, the helicopter, with such ultimate attendant success. (Sikorsky Aircraft)

Above right The one and only **Vought-Sikosky VS-300**, with the 52-year-old, Homburg-hatted Igor Sikorsky at the controls. Taken in late 1939 during one of its early tethered test flights, the machine had two tail rotors at this time, but numerous tail rotor configurations were to be tested before the definitive single rotor layout was chosen. At one point, the VS-300 flew with three rear rotors mounted on what looked like a miniature high-voltage electricity pylon. First flown tethered to the ground by lengthy guy lines on 14 September 1939, the first free flight followed on 13 May 1940. By now the machine could rise vertically, hover and fly backwards, however, almost a year

was to pass before the craft could be induced to fly forward! Redesignated VS-300A at this time, the machine took its final shape in December 1941, when powered by a 100hp Franklin radial. During its evolution, the craft underwent no less than 18 configurational changes and had amassed 102 hours, 35 minutes when it retired from flying in 1943. (Sikorsky Aircraft)

Below The **Doblhoff-WNF WN 342V4**, seen here, was the fourth and last prototype of this the world's first jet-driven, or hot-cycle helicopter. Conceived by the Austrian engineer Friedrich von Doblhoff, the first WN 342 made its maiden flight in the spring of 1943, around six months after development had been initiated. Initially powered by a 60hp With a Mikron to power the air compressor that fed air to the rotor tip combustors, the last WN 342 was a two seater powered by a 140hp BMW Bramo Shl4A. The close-up shows the rotor tip combustor with its internal atomizer ring. Here fuel and compressed air, both fed down the rotor were mixed and ignited by glow plug, the overall unit, with no moving parts, being, in effect, a small, self-starting ramjet. Interestingly, a number of key Doblhoff staff were to continue with their work after the war as employees of the Fairey Aviation Company in Britain, while Doblhoff, himself, went to the US, where he worked with Kellett, later to become Hughes, and McDonnell.

Below The twin intermeshing rotored **Kellett XR-8**, 43.44714, seen here, for the US Army Air Force first flew on 7 August 1944. Powered by a 245hp Franklin 0-405-9, this two man machine had a top speed of 100mph. It did not pass into production. (US Army)

was powered by a single 1,620hp Rolls-Royce Merlin 32 that drove a unique three rotor system. Tragically, VZ 724 was to suffer a catastrophic in-flight failure, commencing in the forward rotor hub, but leading to the disintegration of the starboard rear-rotor support structure. All three crew members, Sqn. Ldr. F.J. 'Jeep' Cable, co-pilot Alan Marsh and flight test observer H.J. Unsworth, losing their lives in the ensuing crash. The second W.11, WA 555, is believed to have been flight tested briefly, but only close to the ground and as part of the investigation into the loss of the first machine. (Cierva)

Development of the **Fairey Gyrodyne** was started at the end of 1945, with the first example, G-AIKF, yet to be carried as seen here, making its first flight on 7 December 1947 at the hands of Fairey Helicopter test pilot, Sqn. Ldr. Basil H. Arkell. The principle behind the Gyrodyne was to use its 520hp Alvis Leonides radial to drive both the main rotor and a pusher propeller mounted on the starboard, or right-hand stub wing – on the second prototype, a tractor propeller was fitted. By the means, the rotor disc loading, aided by the wing lift and propeller thrust was reduced compared with that of a conventional helicopter, promising more speed. That this theory held water was proven on 28 June 1948, when Basil Arkell flew the Gyrodyne at 124.3mph. Sadly, the prototype was to crash on 17 April 1949, following a fatigue failure in the rotor head, killing Fairey's F.H. Dixon and his observer, Derek Garroway. After this, further development of the Gyrodyne ceased, attention shifting to the Jet Gyrodyne. (Fairey Aviation)

The **Hughes XH-17**, 50.1842, was a one-off experimental flying crane heavy-lift helicopter built under US Air Force contract. Utilising the hot-cycle rotor system pioneered by Friedrich von Doblhoff, the output of two 4,000lb s.t. General Electric 7E-TG 180 turbojets was ducted up through the rotor mast and out to a foursome of GE33F combustors near the tip of each rotor blade. Of Interest is the retention of an anti-torque tail rotor on this design, a feature normally rendered unnecessary on helicopters using rotor tip propulsion. With a rotor diameter of 130 feet, the two-man XH-17 made its first flight on 23 October 1952. Maximum load lift capability was 27,000 lbs over 40 miles at a cruising speed of 60mph. (Hughes Aircraft)

The huge three rotored **Cierva W.11 Air Horse** was conceived towards the end of World War II and VZ 724 seen here, the first of two ordered, made its maiden flight on December 8th, 1.948. Developed to meet a need for a heavy-lift helicopter capable of hauling a 5,000lb payload, the W. 11

The sole **Sud Ouest SO 1310 Faradet**, F-W8GD seen here, represented French interest in exploring the potential of the hot-cycle rotored convertiplane comparable to the Fairey Jet Gyrodyne in Britain. For lift-off, compressed air from a 400 ehp Turbomeca Arrius 11 was ducted out to rotor tip combustors. Once aloft the Arrius 11 was shut down and the rotor then went into undriven autorotative mode, with propulsion being provided by the nose-mounted 400shp Turbomeca Marcadau. The Faradet's first untethered flight was made on 8 May 1953, in helicopter form, that is without the nose-mounted Marcadau. With the additional propulsion engine now fitted, the Faradet first flew in full convertiplane mode on 1 July 1953. (GIFAS)

Two **McDonnell XV-1** convertiplanes were built for the US Army, the first of which, 53-4016 is seen here. With Friedrich von Doblhoff heading the XV-1's design team, the machine used the rotor tip combustors Doblhoff had developed for his WN 342 of 1943. Powered by a 550hp Continental R-975-19 radial, the engine output could be switched to power two air compressors that, in turn, fed the rotor tip combustors for vertical lift, or to drive the pusher-mounted propeller for forward flight, at which time the rotor was free to autorotate. First flown on 14 July 1954, the XV-1, on 10 October 1956, became the first rotorcraft to exceed 200mph, actually reaching 203mph. Flight testing of the 2-man XV-1s continued into the late 1950s, by which time it was becoming apparent that conventional helicopters were now promising to overtake the XV-1's major advantage in speed, without the latter's complexity. (McDonnell Aircraft)

Above The sole **Fairey Rotodyne** prototype, XE 521, first flew on 6 November 1957, following a period of exhaustive ground testing that dated back to September 1955. The culmination of a Fairey Aviation programme of convertiplane research initiated at the end of 1945, the Rotodyne was built to meet a 1951 British European Airways specification for a 30 to 40 passenger, vertical take-off and landing 'Bealine Bus'. Powered

by two 3,000shp Napier Eland N.El.3 turboprops with modified auxiliary compressor stages at the rear of the engines from which to draw the rotor system air supply. Just forward of this were clutches that enabled switching the engines from the gas generator mode for take-off and landing, to driving the propellers in cruise. Always destined as a technology demonstrator for a larger 65 passenger, or 75 troop carrying production aircraft, the Rotodyne proved its alacrity on 5 January 1959, when it set a new convertiplane 100 kilometre, or 62 mile closed circuit speed record of 190,897mph in the hands of Fairey's Sqn. Ldr. W.R. Gellatly. Two months after this, New York Airways placed a tentative order for 5, but the take-over of Fairey by Westland, inadequate funding and signs of acoustic fatigue over the next year or two saw interest in the Rotodyne evaporate. (Fairey Aviation)

Evolving the Species, 1909–1955

*T*he preface of this work has already alluded to the fact that aviation development has proven to be extremely sensitive to the economic environment in which it is operating. In times of war, when cash flows fairly freely, the pace of production certainly quickens and this was evidenced in both of the World Wars. However, in both of these cases, while the manufacturing industry's base may have expanded greatly, there was a disproportionately smaller advance in the underlying technology than might have been expected. Put simply, the kind of aircraft and engines available at the start of each major conflict, were, with few exceptions, the kind that were there at the end; they may have grown bigger and faster, with more powerful engines, but the emphasis was always on producing more, rather than to build the new. Thus, World War I produced more powerful biplanes and World War II saw the building of more powerful piston-engined aircraft. Despite the vast cash injections going into aviation for the Great War, only a handful of Fokker and Junkers monoplane fighters were to come into service and even fewer of the latter with their all-metal construction. Similarly, in World War II, the advent of the first operational jet fighters, Messerschmitt's Me 262 and the

Gloster Meteor by mid-1944, did not signal a decisive switch from the production of such existing piston-engined types as the Supermarine Spitfire, Hawker Tempest, Messerschmitt Bf 109 or North American P-51 Mustang. Major wars, it would appear, see the emphasis being placed firmly on quantity, rather than quality. (Though admittedly, jet technology must have been accelerated by desperation in Germany.)

In the light of the above observations, it follows that the mass of truly innovative aviation developments tend to happen during periods of economic slow-down or even recession and there is much evidence, including some in this section, to prove the case. Sadly, the implication of this, all too frequently borne out by events, is that innovations often take a long time, or even worse, some innovations prove to be stillborn because they lack the necessary financial support. However, even in such cases, all is not always lost, but simply delayed until someone else happens along, learns of the potential breakthrough and incorporates the earlier thinking into their own efforts. The aviation design community has a long and successful track record of mimicking good ideas, a practice that, at least, tends to stop people from constantly attempting to re-invent the wheel.

Below The large aircraft was no longer a rarity by the end of World War I, thanks largely to the pioneering work of Sikorsky, Caproni, Handley Page and Farman. In this context, the often overlooked, short-lived **Zeppelin Staaken** E.4250, designed under the leadership of Adolf Rohrbach, deserves more than a fleeting mention. Starting life in 1918 as one of the new breed of German monoplane bombers, the four engined E.4250 was rapidly transformed into an airliner in the wake of the Armistice. Reported to have been briefly test flown towards the end of 1919, there were some indications that the machine was overweight for its total installed power. That may well have been the case, after all, such shortfalls were not that uncommon then, or, for that matter, for many years to come. What must be recognised is the visionary design approach of Rohrbach, who, taking the best of Hugo Junkers' and Claudius Dornier's innovations, came up with this magnificent design signpost to the classic high wing, monoplane airliner formula that was to be adopted by Fokker in Holland and by such Americans as 'Bill' Stout for his AT series and 'Jack' Northrop, for his Lockheed Vega design of 1928. Rohrbach's adoption of all-metal construction took longer to become universally accepted, with others following by the mid-1920s in the US; but it took about a decade longer in the case of all but a few of the more far-sighted European manufacturers. (US National Archives)

The extremely bird-like two seat **Etrich Taube**, or Pidgeon, that first flew in November 1909 was to become Europe's most successful aircraft in the period prior to World War I, certainly in terms of numbers built. Designed by the Austrian, Igo Etrich, the original Taube was powered by an 85hp Austro-Daimler in-line engine, as seen here. Note the complexity of rigging and control wires employed on this aircraft, that relied on wing warping, rather than ailerons. Popular from the outset with pilots because of its easy handling, the Taube had already sold in some numbers when in 1911 its order book was to receive an instant boost, following the type's selection as Germany's standard two-seat reconnaissance and training aircraft. Ultimately, around 500 examples were to be licence-built in Germany alone, by a number of manufacturers led by Rumpler. Progressively re-engined with various types of up to 120hp, the Taube stayed in front-line service until well into 1915, while, as a trainer, the type was still in use in 1916.

Despite aviation still being in its comparative infancy, progress by 1913 was little short of explosive. One such development was the emergence of the really large aircraft, in, of all places, Russia, closely followed by the designs of Caproni in Italy. For once, in this period of French domination of aviation developments in general, the honour of producing the world's first truly large aircraft goes to Russia and Igor Sikorsky's **Ilya Mourometz** series of four-engined giants. Between 1914 and

mid to late 1917, Russia was to produce eighty of these huge machines, the power output of whose engines rose individually from 100 to 220hp in the later machines. When equipped with the 220hp Renault engine, the bomber's top level speed with a 1,120lb bombload was a leisurely 75mph, which would, at first glance, infer their vulnerability to attack. Evidently, this was not the case as the record shows only one of these machines to have been downed in combat, and that only after it had accounted for three of its assailants! Flight duration of these four-engined 'heavies' was said to be 6 hours, which suggests a tactical radius of action with a useful bombload of around 150 miles. (Sikorsky Aircraft)

Professor Hugo Junkers, the engineer, industrialist, but primarily researcher, portrayed here in his later years. Already a successful industrialist by the end of the 1890s, Hugo Junkers could be counted among the handful of manufacturers of that time who provided basic welfare services for his workforce. This was to alienate him in the eyes of the Nazis in his later life. During the early years of this century, Hugo Junkers turned his research talents to aviation, setting up a wind tunnel-equipped research institute in Aachen. One of the early fruits of this research took the form of a visionary 1910 patent for a large, thick-wing-section flying wing transport aircraft: virtually everything was housed within a smooth, fully cantilevered

structure. Junkers then turned to all-metal aircraft construction and set up an aircraft design organisation under Otto Reuter. This effort culminated in the F 13, generally considered to be the precursor of the modern, all-metal airliner. A true polymath, Junkers, not content to rest on his laurels, used the 1920s to expand successfully into a number of areas: ranging from establishing airline affiliations across the globe to setting up an aero-engine company that, among other things, developed an impressive diesel aircraft engine used to power some of Blohm und Voss's and Dornier's long-range seaplanes, as well as his own JU 86 series. Regrettably, his perceived 'socialist tendencies' were intolerable to the Nazi regime when it came to power in early 1933 and little time was lost in removing him from control of his own industrial empire. Hugo Junkers, died soon after, a broken man, on 3 February 1935, his 76th birthday. (Junkers AG)

Above The sole, all-metal **Junkers J-1** was always intended as a pure research aircraft with its second seat specifically set aside for a flight test observer. Thanks to its fully cantilevered wing and tail unit bereft of the need for any form of external strut or wire bracing, the J-1 was an exceptionally clean looking machine. It could be seen as the first major milestone between the wood-and-wire era and that of the modern aircraft, a transition that Junkers contributed to more than any other. This said, it must be noted that the J-1 was anything but a success in itself, as the Junkers team's approach to structural design owed far more to established bridge building, than aeronautical, practices. Built of steel, the machine was almost certainly extremely robust, but it incurred an all-up-weight penalty that almost stopped vital military financial support at the start. First flown on 12 December 1915, the J-1 was soon being evaluated against the Rumpler C 1, considered to be the finest of the contemporary military two seaters. While the J-1, at 106mph, was 7mph faster than the Rumpler, it was distinctly poorer in terms of climb and agility - two very important yardsticks in the minds of military aviators then and now. Despite these shortfalls, the military decided to continue development of the Junkers all-metal monoplane series, which staggered on through the J-2 and J-7, perceived as 'disasters', before the successful emergence of the J-8/1D 1 and J-9/C1 1 machines in 1918. (Junkers AG)

Above right Clearly ahead of its time, the fascinating **Gotha**-built **Ursinus** single-seat floatplane fighter never progressed beyond the sole prototype. Powered by a 150hp Benz, the machine was designed during the latter part of 1915. Central to the Ursinus concept was the use of the two retractable main floats, that, once aloft, tucked up to form the aircraft's belly to reduce drag by a considerable amount, along

with providing a buoyant hull in the case of an emergency forced landing on water. Just how good this machine would have proved from an operational stand-point remains a matter of conjecture, as the fighter was lost during flight testing in 1916. Somewhat surprisingly for a young industry that was usually quite quick to pick up on good ideas, only two subsequent aircraft proposed for production, the Blackburn B-20 of 1940 and Convair's XF2Y-1 Seadart of 1953, were to employ a comparable form of float retraction.

The Sopwith Pup (overleaf) was genuinely liked by its Royal Navy and Royal Flying Corps pilots for its agility and friendly handling qualities. It was this ease of handling that the Royal Navy sought to exploit when they put Pups aboard both cruisers and the early aircraft carriers during the first half of 1917. Shown here is one of the skid-equipped **Sopwith 9901A Pups**, aimed at improving carrier deck landing and development of which culminated in flight trials aboard HMS *Furious* during

April 1917. In the event, this cumbersome looking and dangerous apology for a landing system was abandoned in favour of the
conventional wheeled type. One sea-going Pup, launched from a
20-ft-long platform on the light cruiser, HMS *Yarmouth*, did
manage to carve a niche in the annals of military aviation, when,
on 21 August 1917, in the hands of Sub Lieutenant B.A. Smart,
it shot down Zeppelin L.23. (Crown Copyright)

Right Frederick Handley Page, later to be knighted, was among the
first to realise the advantages of the slotted wing, a feature that
allowed the aircraft either to fly slower for a given weight, or
to lift-off at a higher weight without stalling – avoiding that
frequently literal sinking feeling when an aircraft quits flying.
Following a series of patents granted Handley Page in late
October 1919, his company acquired this war-surplus Puma-
engined DH 9 in February 1920, modifying it as the **Handley
Page HP 17**, with leading edge slots fitted to both upper and
lower wings. Seen here in its earliest form, a longer, stronger
set of landing gear legs were later fitted, in April 1920. These
trials had an enormous impact on the aviation world, with the
HP 17 demonstrating a 30% improvement in the peak amount
of wing lift produced by the use of slots. (Handley Page)

Opposite, above right The **Dayton Wright XPS-1**, seen here,
represented the radical approach to applied research, as
opposed to the evolutionary path chosen by Handley Page with
his HP 17. Whereas Handley Page tested a single, albeit
significant, development aboard an otherwise tried and tested
airframe and engine combination, Dayton Wright elected to
carry all of their innovative eggs in one basket. What was all the
more surprising about the XPS-1 is that Dayton Wright, of all

people, should have known better. The XPS-1 was, in essence, little more than an improved Rhinehart-Baumann RB-1, built by the company for the 1920 James Gordon Bennett race. Both used the same interlocked system of landing gear retraction and wing camber alteration that could seldom be made to work properly. If nothing else, all three XPS-1s built simply demonstrated that the one thing a military aircraft needs to be is reliable. (U.S Air Force)

The extremely handsome **Westland Dreadnought** postal monoplane, of which only one example, J6.986, was built. Seen here at Westland's Yeovil airfield prior to its first and only flight of 9 May 1923, the Dreadnought incorporated a blended wing/fuselage structure and was powered by a 450hp Napier Lion II with accommodation for two pilots and up to eight passengers, or the equivalent in mail. Certainly, in comparison with contemporaries, the Dreadnought appeared to look the

part. However, the Dreadnought was to prove spectacularly unsuccessful: shortly after take-off the machine stalled and crashed, maiming its test pilot, Stuart Keep. A contributory factor was the use of a low-set, knife-sharp leading edge to the wing's airfoil section, something calculated to make any stall just that little bit more vicious. Despite the Dreadnought's fate, the blended wing/fuselage concept has re-surfaced on several occasion since, with the Miles Y series, McDonnell's XP-67 and most recently in the General Dynamics originated F-16. (Westland)

Right The incredibly ugly **Armstrong Whitworth Ape** was conceived by the scientists of the Royal Aircraft Establishment, Farnborough, as a modular in-flight adjustable aerodynamic and

Inset **Georg Wulf**, who, with Prof. Heinrich Focke, founded the Bremen-based Focke-Wulf Flugzeugbau in January 1924. (via Hans Justus Meier)

craft handling test vehicle. Clearly, they should have known
ºtter. As seen here in this view of J 7754, the second of
ºree Apes built, the tailplane incidence could be altered
ºramatically. Provision was made to alter momen-arm forces by
ºding or subtracting sections of the fuselage on either side of
ºe two-man centre section. Grossly underpowered with a
ºOhp Armstrong Siddeley Lynx III and first flown on 5 January
º26, the three Apes proved to be almost totally useless, J 7754
ºashing on 23 May 1929. Shortly after this, the previously
ºoradic use of these machines was abandoned, but not before
ºesumably the same RAE scientists that had dreamt the whole
ºing up had conducted a protracted review of why the Ape
ºd demonstrated such an abysmal performance.
ºrmstrong Whitworth)

Below left The **Focke-Wulf F19A Ente**, D 1960, seen here
shortly after completion in 1930 with, on the left, Prof. Heinrich
Focke and company chief pilot Edzard. Often during this period,
such things as the A suffix to the design number inferred
nothing more drastic than some slight modification, or engine
upgrade to the same machine. Not so in the case of the F19,
where the A actually signifies radical, if not immediately obvious
changes to the aircraft – a point lost on a number of latter-day
commentators, who are clearly unaware of the existence of the
first F19. First flown on 2 September 1927, the F19 canard
was aimed at the still embryonic air taxi/feederliner market and, as
such, carried a pilot and up to three passengers. Powered by
two 75hp Siemens Halske Sh II radials, the F19 cruised at 80mph
and incorporated one quite novel purported safety feature that
was to lead to the death of Georg Wulf, Director, Chief Pilot and
co-founder of the company. Included within the parasol
mounted foreplane of the F19 was a pivoting mechanism that
allowed the foreplane to tilt side-to-side. The purpose of this
tilting foreplane, according to the patent held by Prof. Focke, was
to ease pilot control problems in the case of losing an engine.
According to one knowledgeable source at the time, this tilting
device had one drawback, it did not work in one particular set
of circumstances. Apparently aware of this flaw, Georg Wulf, who
had thoroughly tested the F19 over the past three weeks, took
it aloft for a demonstration flight in front of potential buyers on
29 September 1927. During the course of this demonstration,
made at low level, Wulf encountered whatever the problem was
and although he nearly retrieved flying speed and control, the
machine struck the ground killing him. The second machine, the
F19A could be readily differentiated from the first by its
underwing fins. Not so immediately apparent was the absence
of the tilting mechanism from the now fixed foreplane. Thus
modified, the sole F19A was to continue flying throughout the
1930s, ultimately retiring in 1939. (VFW)

The sad story of the **Handley Page HP 39 Gugnunc** is a
case of a bruised ego pouring good money after bad in what
always looked to be a futile exercise. First flown on 30 April
1929, the sole HP 39, G-AACN, was built specifically to
compete in the US-based Guggenheim Safe Aircraft
Competition, which Frederick Handley Page felt would be a
great showcase for his likely winner of a design. This was not to
be the case, for after some protracted wrangling the declared
winner was the Curtiss Tanager, the HP 39 being unplaced. This

somewhat dubious result even engendered critical comment from parts of the American aviation press. Meanwhile, a disgruntled Handley Page involved the company in spending additional sums to those already incurred on the US trip, by taking out a lawsuit against Curtiss for non-payment of royalties for what Handley Page considered were his patented wing slots. This judgement would also go against him. Seen here being flown by J. Cordes from the company's Cricklewood airfield in June 1929, the HP 39 was powered by a 150hp Armstrong Siddeley Mongoose and had an impressive speed range of 112.5 to 33.5mph. (Handley Page)

Inset Born in 1895, **John Knudson 'Jack' Northrop** migrated with his family from the US east coast to California in 1904 and it was here, in 1916, that Jack Northrop joined the Loughead Brothers, later to become Lockheed. By 1919, Jack Northrop had designed his first aircraft, the Loughead S-1, a smart looking sports biplane. The big problem with the S-1 was its $2,500 price tag, at a time when war-surplus Curtiss JNs were selling for $400, which helps explain why the Loughead concern went out of business in 1920. After a three-year break from aviation, Jack joined the Douglas Company in 1923, rejoining the reformed Lockheed, as it then was, in 1927. It was at this time that Jack Northrop designed the famed Lockheed Vega, but, restless to set up his own company, left in 1928, aided by Ken Jay, to establish the Avion Corporation. It was while heading Avion that Jack Northrop developed the all-metal, multi-cellular sparred wing that was later to serve the Douglas DC series so well. Others of Jack's designs at this time included the beautiful Alpha single-engined, low wing monoplane and the so-called Flying Wing. In the wake of the Great Depression, Avion was absorbed into Stearman during 1932 and Jack went into partnership with Donald Douglas to form the Northrop arm of Douglas between 1932 and 1938, which became the El Segundo Division of Douglas when Jack left to once more attempt to go it alone. Establishing the present Northrop, now Northrop Grumman, in August 1939, Jack was to produce not only his series of flying wings, but also such formidable all-weather fighters as the P-61 Black Widow and F-89 Scorpion. Jack Northrop retired in 1952 and, shortly before his death in 1981, was invited back to the company he had founded to be shown details of the Northrop B-2 stealth flying wing bomber ordered by the US Air Force in late 1980. (Northrop)

Main image Not quite, but a clear pointer to the family of flying wings that Jack Northrop would devote so much of his latter years to developing, the so-called **Avion Flying Wing** of 1929. A half-way stage between the aerodynamically clean, but otherwise conventional Lockheed Vega that Northrop had designed in 1927 and the as yet to be conceived series of 1940s flying wings, this purely experimental type, registered as X-216H, was powered by a 90hp flat four Menasco and was flown first as a pusher, then as a tractor-engined machine on numerous occasions in the period 1929-1930. (Northrop)

Overleaf The sole, diminutive **Parnall Prawn**, S 1576, seen here at the Air Ministry's Marine Aircraft Experimental Establishment, Felixstowe in 1930. Going one better than the World War I Ursinus design, the Prawn boasted a propeller and propeller shaft, inclinable through either 10.9 or 22 degrees

from the normal thrust line, in order to keep the airscrew from striking the water. To compound a set of problems strictly of the designer's own making, the 65hp Richardo-Burt powered single-seat flying boat sported a four-bladed propeller of such minuscule diameter that it looked more suited to a rotary garden mower than an aircraft. Understandably, perhaps, this unlikely combination of engine, transmission and propeller proved totally inadequate to the task of pulling the Prawn through the water at any respectable speed, let alone of dragging it aloft. (Air Ministry, Crown Copyright)

Below First flown in March 1936, the **Gérin Varivol** was one of the more radical attempts to expand an aircraft's speed range, a capability that appeared particularly to exercise the French during the 1930s. Broaden the speed range for a given weight and the machine flies faster and lands slower, the latter a major safety bonus. Jacques Gérin's approach was to design a machine with tiny wings, little more than leading edges in fact, married to a roller-blind style deployable, flexible curved surface that made up the body of the wing surface. Made of a rubberised material with spring steel aided curvature, the surface could be rolled in to minimise drag, or fully extended to provide maximum lift at low speed and touch down. Powered by a 230hp Salmson radial, the Varivol, (Variable Wing), flew on a number of occasions between March and 29 November 1936, when the machine crashed, killing its pilot. However, according to contemporary reports the crash was not connected with the novel wing. French Government wind tunnel testing of the Gérin wing mated to a modified, single engined Caudron continued during and immediately after World War II.

Right Variations on a **Lysander** theme I. (Actually post-dating that below.) Westlands, at the close of 1940, were still producing Lysanders at a good rate, this despite the fact that the Germans now occupied most of the places a Lysander could be used. In the circumstances, the only surprise, if anything, was that there were not more experimental Lysanders than ultimately emerged. One interesting modification was made to Lysander II, P 9105, which was fitted with the high-lift Blackburn-Steiger wing with its full-span flaps. This constant chord wing reduced the wingspan from the standard 50 feet to 38 feet. This new wing carried a forward sweep of nine degrees to ensure the machine's handling remained satisfactory. (Westland)

Variations on a **Westland Lysander** theme II. During the spring of 1940 Westlands received an Air Ministry requirement to investigate the possibility of equipping the Lysander to take a rear-mounted, powered gun turret. Intrigued with results published by Maurice Delanne for his tandem-winged light aircraft, W.E.W. Petter, Westland's Technical Director, had Harold Penrose, the company's chief test pilot, fly him over to France to be briefed by Delanne. Penrose flew the tandem-winged machine and both men returned home impressed and with the solution to their problem. In due course the prototype Lysander, K 6127. emerged, modified to take a Delanne-style rear wing, plus fully weighted rear turret mock-up. As often occurred at this time, by the time Penrose took the drastically altered Lysander aloft for the first time on 27 July 1941, the need for it had evaporated. In flight, the Delanne Lysander proved a highly stable and docile machine which, according to reports, Penrose took aloft whenever possible, causing much confusion among the local aircraft spotters. (Westland)

Right Conceived as a six-crewed maritime patrol bomber, the design of the sole **Blackburn B.20**, V 8914, commenced in 1937, but was not completed until 1939. As can be seen, the B.20 employed a retractable central float, plus two smaller retractable wing tip floats in a manner that wedded the best of the 1915 Ursinus and the 1935 Consolidated PBY-1. With these drag-reducing devices and under the power of its two 1,720hp Rolls-Royce Vulture Xs, the estimated top level speed for the B.20 was put at an impressive 306mph at 15,000 feet. The estimated operational range of this eight .303-inch gunned flying boat was 1,500 miles with a bomb or depth charge load of two 500lb weapons carried in two inboard wing bays. The promise of the B.20 was to prove illusory. A few days after its end of

March first flight, the one and only B.20 was to crash and be destroyed as a result of suffering high speed aileron flutter. The only positive part of the outcome was that the pilot, Flt. Lt. H. Bailey, killed in the crash, fought to control the aircraft long enough to allow the other two crew members to parachute safely from the stricken machine. (Blackburn)

The mammoth 212 feet wingspan sole **Douglas XB-19**, 38-741, holds a crowd of Douglas workers enthralled as it taxies away from its Santa Monica birthplace to depart for the nearby US Army Air Corps base at March Field on its 27 June

1941 first flight. Initiated at the US Army's behest in early 1935, the XB-19 was never intended to enter production; rather it was always destined to serve as a test bed to see just how far existing technology could be pushed. The biggest problem was lack of money, causing the planned debut of the XB-19 to slip by more than three years. Powered by four 2,000hp Wright R-3350-5s, the bomber's top level speed was 224mph at 15,700 feet, while the giant cruised at 135mph. These were not particularly impressive figures for 1941, but the 7,300 mile range with a 6,000lb bombload surely was. (Douglas Aircraft)

The **Miles M.30 X Minor**, U-0233, was a one-off, small scale prototype first flown in February 1942 to test the blended wing/fuselage four- and six-engined airliner concepts drawn up by F. G. Miles in the late 1930s. The M.30 ended its relatively brief career as an instructional airframe with the Miles Aeronautical Technical school, Shown inset is the 50 passenger **Miles X 11** project of 1943. Performance estimates indicated the X 11 would cruise at 350mph and have a range of 3,450 miles with a full passenger complement. With Miles always considered something of an industry outsider, the X 11 proposal was spurned by officialdom in favour of what was to become the Bristol Britannia. (Miles)

Another one-off, the **Miles M.35 Libellula**, or dragonfly, U-0235, seen here being flown by George, the younger of the flying Miles Brothers. George's brainchild, the M.35 was designed and assembled within a six week period and kept under wraps from the possible prying eyes of government officials, lest they veto this unconventional, low speed, low powered test vehicle for a proposed deck-landing fighter. Lacking any wind tunnel testing that would have alerted the

men from the ministry, George was to fly the ground-hugging canard for the first time on 1 May 1942: and probably instantly regretted it, as the aircraft promptly proved to be inherently unstable around its pitching axis when eventually coaxed aloft This problem remained with the M.35, being only partially alleviated by the use of ballast. As the larger and later M.39 canard was to show, the 130hp DH Gipsy Major-powered M.35's troubles lay not with its back-to-front layout, but with the lack of pre-flight wind tunnel testing. (Miles)

Vought's V-173 was dubbed the 'flying pancake' the instant it was glimpsed by the press. The brainchild of former NACA aerodynamicist, Charles H. Zimmerman. this one-off prototype was built to flight test the potential of a low aspect ratio, or low span to chord wing, fully immersed in propeller wash Zimmerman, incidentally, had already proved much of his concept with a series of small flying scale models. Following it first flight on 23 November 1942, with Vought's Chief of Flight Test, Boone T. Guyton at the controls, the V-173 went on to amass over 131 hours aloft. A spectacularly short take-off performer, the V-173 'unstuck' after a mere 200 feet, climbing away at a steep angle. Flying into a headwind of 29mph, the V-173 would rise vertically away from the ground. The V-173's landing roll was equally dramatic, frequently taking as little as 50 feet to come to rest from touch down. Powered by two 80hp Continental A-80s, what must have caused those flying the machine some concern was what would happen in the case of an engine failure, as the V-173's engines were not cross-shafted to maintain some power to both propellers. (Vought)

From the same brain that gave the world the Douglas DC-3 this E.F. Burton conception for a DH Mosquito-style fast day bomber stemmed from an early 1943 company-funded study. With its twin 1,325hp Allison V-1710-93s housed side-by-side

within the fuselage and driving pusher contra-rotating propellers via a gearbox and extension shaft, the two-man **Douglas XB-42** was the subject of a June 1943 US Army Air Force contract, involving the building of two examples. This curious pusher type first flew on 6 May 1944, and could reach a top level speed of 410mph at 23,440 feet. Cruising at around 312mph, the range was 1,840 miles with a bombload of 8,000lb Shown here is the second example, 43.50225. The XB-42 evolved into the jet-powered XB-43. (Douglas Aircraft)

Below **McDonnell** Aircraft were another to explore the virtues of the blended wing/fuselage idea with their twin 1,350hp Continental XI-1430-1711,9 powered **XP-67** single seat fighter. First flown on 6 January 1944, already a month behind target as a result of engine problems, the XP-67's flight testing was constantly being delayed by engine troubles, the only example, 42-11677, ultimately being lost on 6 September 1944, as a direct result of an in-flight engine fire. With these troublesome, under-developed engines and a quite poor top level speed of 405mph at 25,000 feet, it is extremely improbable that the XP-67 would have ever passed into production. The one thing the XP-67 did have in its favour was its armament of six 37mm cannons, the heaviest of its day. Ironically, the construction of a second XP-67 equipped with twin Packard-built Rolls-Royce Merlins was nearly complete when the US Army Air Force withdrew support. (McDonnell Aircraft)

A new viewpoint on a 'wooden wonder'. One interesting, if off-beat research tool was this re-nosed **Airspeed Horsa** used to check the effective crew visibility out of the yet to be built De Havilland DH 106 Comet. Modified to take the new nose in January 1947, flight testing of this wooden construction hybrid was undertaken by John Cunningham, whose tug was a Handley Page Halifax A 7. In order to experience worst case conditions, much of the testing, necessarily, was undertaken in rain or

snow. That not all modification work is done inside heated hangars is evident from the inset picture of a snow covered Hatfield aerodrome during one of the bleakest British winters on record. (De Havilland)

Bottom The idea of producing a car that flies has been around for a long time, Glenn Curtiss had built an Aerocar in 1917. It did not generate mass market appeal then or since, but, nonetheless, the appeal of the concept appears to have been addictive to more than one designer, as is seen with these two post-World War II examples. This is the sole **Convair Model 118**, NX.90850, intended to be the production version of the Convair Model 116 prototype first flown on 12 July 1946. During the latter part of 1946, this technology demonstrator made 66 flights. At this juncture, it might have been prudent to put a hold on development effort and take time out to ask if there were any buyers for an aerocar. As history shows, there weren't; but much time and effort clearly went into producing a stylishly glossy product in the shape of the Model 118. Powered by a 190hp Lycoming 0-435C for flying, the two seat car carried its own engine for road use. First flown from Lindburgh Field, San Diego on 15 November 1947, the Model 118 failed to arouse even lukewarm market interest and it, along with its very senior designer/advocate were both quietly abandoned in late 1948. (Convair)

Right The other example of someone with a fixation on combining wheels with wings is that of Moulton Taylor, the founder of the Aerocar company in February 1948. Taylor's approach differed from that of Convair's in as much as Taylor's series of Aerocars all used the one engine for both airborne and road use. Between October 1949 and the mid to late 1950s, Taylor flew and demonstrated his Aerocars I, II and III, all two seaters with installed power rising from 100hp to 135hp and ultimately 160hp. In performance terms the **Aerocar III**

combining gearbox. This type of turboprop had particular appeal to naval forces, who saw the advantages of eliminating take-off torque reaction from a confined flight deck as a marvellous plus point. As a bonus, they could shut down one of the units in cruise flight to economise on fuel. In Britain, the Royal Navy already had Westland developing the Wyvern by the end of World War II, albeit in piston engined form, using the Rolls-Royce Eagle. What could be simpler than changing engine from piston to turboprop? As it turned out, the desk-bound naval warrior's 'chop and change' approach failed, with the usual British procurement vacillations complicating more fundamental problems concerning the development of the generic turboprop, and deadlines were not met. The first turbo-proppowered Wyvern, the TF 2, took to the air on 18 January 1949, this with the 4,030eshp Rolls-Royce Cyde. Even before this flight, it had long been decided to put the Wyvern into production, as the TF 4, using the 4,110eshp Armstrong Siddeley Python. First flown with the Python on 22 March 1949, the TF 4 was reluctantly given its restricted service release over four years later, in May 1953. Incidentally, the intervening and protracted development programme that was predominantly propulsion-centred, was strewn with fatal crashes. Propulsion troubles continued to plague the Wyvern to the end, most flying from shore prior to an early service withdrawal in March 1958. (Westland)

The huge single-seat **Douglas XA2D-1 Skyshark** was one of only two front-line turboprop combat types to enter development within the US, both for the US Navy and both failing to get into production. Like its twin-engined North American XA2J-1 contemporary, the Skyshark used the 5,100eshp Allison XT40-A-2, itself a coupling of two XT38 driving a combining gearbox. As with the Westland Wyvern, it was strictly the engine, not the airframe that was the trouble. First flown on 26 May 1950, by Douglas Project Pilot, George Jansen, the prototype, Bu Aer 122988, seen here, was to be

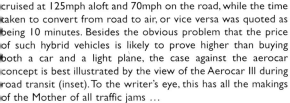

cruised at 125mph aloft and 70mph on the road, while the time taken to convert from road to air, or vice versa was quoted as being 10 minutes. Besides the obvious problem that the price of such hybrid vehicles is likely to prove higher than buying both a car and a light plane, the case against the aerocar concept is best illustrated by the view of the Aerocar III during road transit (inset). To the writer's eye, this has all the makings of the Mother of all traffic jams ...

The **Westland Wyvern TF 4** seen here was the only production turboprop fighter to be built, not just in Britain, but the world. It was an ill-starred venture from the beginning. However, before reviewing the Wyvern and its closest US contemporary, the need for a turboprop front-line combat aircraft in the post-World War II jet era, must be considered. The turboprop engine may have had its limitations in terms of out-and-out speed as the propeller tips encountered compressibility shock, but it was lightweight and powerful. This aspect of the turboprop had been grasped by would-be engine producers by the early 1940s, some time before the first flight-worthy units existed. One particular design approach that found favour first in the US, was to couple two turboprops together to drive contra-rotating propellers through a destroyed just short of eight months later, killing the Navy's Project Pilot, Lt. Cdr. Hugh Woods, following the break-up of one of the coupled units' turbine stages Similar problems were besetting the XA2J-1. However, whereas the Royal Navy chose to persevere, the US Navy soon abandoned both of these carrier-going turboprop attack types. There was, at least for the Americans, a silver lining to their turboprop cloud, as the passing of the Skyshark left Douglas's Ed Heinmann free to busy himself with yet another Navy attack type, the A4D, later A-4 Skyhawk, a design by which others of its class would be judged for the next thirty years. (Douglas Aircraft)

Right This **North American** publicity photograph, taken on 29 September 1954, of the hand-over of the first **F-100As** to their US Air Force users, is a stark reminder of a problem that was about to shake the company and kill a number of unsuspecting pilots. George Welsh, Chief of Flight Test for North American had been flying the two prototype YF-100As since the type's first flight on 25 May 1953 and, during these sixteen months, found nothing of fundamental concern. However, within weeks of the first service hand-overs, Tactical Air Command started to lose F-100As and their pilots in seemingly inexplicable crashes. North American and Welsh were called in to investigate. On 12 October 1954, George Welsh was killed when the F-100A he was flying broke up due to the phenomenon of roll-coupling, little understood at that time outside of the small, elite group of Edwards AFB X plane pilots. The reason for the sudden onset of F-100A losses lay in the fins of these production machines, which had been shortened from those of the two development aircraft. A reversion to the original, taller fin cured the problem. (North American)

Below The desire on the part of some people to hang aeroplanes from things including cables, balloons, airships and other aeroplanes goes back to the very early years of powered flight. Shown here, is one of the last serious attempts made to do this by, of all people, the USAF, who actually deployed a limited number of **Republic RF-84K**-carrying **Convair GRB-36Ds** operationally from the end of 1956, through most of 1957. Shown here and taken in May 1953 is a view of the operational evaluation trials involving a Convair GRB-36F and a Republic YRF-84F. The intention with this particular combination was not to carry some form of fighter protection for the mother aircraft, but to extend the range of the Air Forces' photographic reconnaissance capability by using the mother ship to fly the fast RF-84 to within credible fuel range of what was to be photographed. The arrival in service of the fast, longer-ranged Douglas RB-66s must have come as a relief to those tasked with operating the by now extremely vulnerable GRB-36s. (US Air Force)

The Tailless Option, 1906–1952

*D*uring the years immediately prior to World War II probably the most appealing of all plane designs were the alluringly smooth, beautifully proportioned high performance flying wing sailplanes produced by the Horten Brothers, Reimar and Walter, in Germany. These elegantly sculpted craft carried a universal appeal. To the artistic their shape and proportions appeared graceful, while their aerodynamic appearance appealed to the more technical minds. However, those few pilots of this period that had flown tailless types viewed them in an entirely different light. Two generic handling problems characterised tailless aircraft of all shapes and sizes. First, lacking the fuselage-provided moment arm that a conventional aircraft's elevators have, pitch axis, or nose-up, nose-down control was always going to be a problem and this usually manifested itself in an over-sensitivity in pitch control. The other seemingly universal characteristic of tailless types was their lack of directional stability. Understandably, the less the fin area employed by the designer, the more acute this tendency to yaw from side to side away from the desired straight line flight path. This strong diversion of opinion between the flyers and non-flyers, and among aircraft designers, was not confined to tailless types, but it certainly appears to have been more marked and lasted longer with this class of aircraft than with any other. There are two important reasons why, (among others). First, do not underestimate the power of human obsession. 'Jack' Northrop's involvement with his line of flying wings appears to have bordered on the obsessive, while such was the Horten Brothers' intensity of focus on this one type of aircraft that they spent most of World War II finding new ways of obtaining German Air Ministry funding to support their researches into their special brand of sailplane. Secondly, do not underestimate the room for error in communiction between the aeronautical researcher and the aircraft constructor. The lack of communication between the RAE and De Havilland, for example, ensured that the DH 108 was a disaster, costing several lives, including that of Sir Geoffrey's son. The RAE failed to pass on its reservations about Taylor's designs to the industry.

The case of the DH 108 highlights a problem that tended to creep up on designers of the faster tailless aircraft of the 1940s. Almost universally, as airspeeds increased pitch control effectiveness fell off and the aircraft would go into progressively more violent pitching oscillation. In some instances, these oscillations were at such a frequency as to get out of phase with the pilot's reactions, a state of affairs referred to as Pilot Induced Oscillation. With PIO, the pilot found himself unwittingly making things worse when his control input, lagging behind the pitching state of the machine, only amplified the severity of the pitching. The advent of the post-World War II family of delta-winged aircraft, coupled with second-generation powered flight control systems, helped alleviate this problem.

The creation of French-born, English domiciled Jose Weiss, the **Weiss Glider** of 1909 was the product of model flight testing over many years. This glider, that successfully carried Gordon English aloft, embodied swept-back wings, along with a smooth canoe-style, underslung body fore-shadowing by many years the designs of Capt., later Prof. G.T.R. Hill in Britain and the efforts of Alexander Lippisch and the Horten Brothers in Germany. Note the turn table-mounted launching ramp topped with weather vane. (Cowin Collection)

The tailless designs produced by Lt., later Major, John W. Dunne for the British War Office between 1906 and 1913 are frequently cited as being the first flyable tailless aircraft to emerge. All were characterised by carrying a pronounced degree of sweep-back to their wings. Dunne's efforts, it should be noted, were aimed solely at producing a safer flying machine, endowed with the highest degree of inherent stability possible and some of Dunne's ingenuity in this area foreshadowed the primitive auto-pilots of the 1930s. Here, the **Dunne D.6** of 1910, powered by a 50hp Green engine, is being demonstrated to no less a personage than Wilbur Wright, accompanied by Griffith Brewer, during their visit to Eastchurch on 20 December 1910.

Capt., later Prof. Geoffrey T. R. Hill's **Westland Pterodactyl Ib**, first flown in mid-June 1928, was, perhaps, the most visually pleasing of this series of tailless aircraft produced by Westland under his design leadership. A former chief test pilot for Handley Page, the Capt.ain had devoted much of his efforts during the 1921 to 1924 period attempting to devise a safe, stall-proof aircraft. Aided by a 3-year research scholarship and subsequent support from the Royal Aircraft Establishment, Hill brought forth his first tailless glider at the end of 1924 and, built with the aid of RAE, a much improved powered version in the autumn of 1925. Hill joined Westland during the spring of 1926, where he embarked on the design of the machine shown here, which carried the Air Ministry serial J9251. This machine in its

Mk. Ib form was powered by a 70hp Armstrong Siddeley Genet mounted as a pusher. From the outset of flight trials with this machine it showed a marked propensity for flying along in a series of up and down oscillations rather than remaining level, a trait that may well have been aided by Hill's use of more than ample aero-isoclinic controls. In this system the wingtips swivel around the main spar to provide pitch control if used in unison, or roll control if used differentially. Top speed was 70mph. (Westland)

Westland, following upon the Pterodactyl experience, elected to forego the Mk. II and III projected tailless fighters in favour of the more modest **Mk. IV** three-seater research vehicle. The sole example, K 1947, first flew in June 1931 and was powered by a 120hp DH Gipsy III. The Mk. IV's maximum achievable speed in level flight was 113mph. Interestingly, in an effort to cure the roller-coaster excursions of the Mk. I, Capt. Hill reverted to using elevons on the Mk. IV, in place of swivelling wingtip, but the pitch control problems appear to have remained unaffected. (Westland)

1931 was the year in which it seemed the estimable Capt. Hill's efforts were to be rewarded, when his two-seat **Pterodactyl Mk. V** proposals gained Air Ministry acceptance, with the one proviso that the machine be powered by a 600hp Rolls-Royce PV.G, later known as the Goshawk. With the relevant paperwork completed, work on the sole Mk. V, K 2770, commenced in early 1932, against Air Ministry Specification F.3132. Completed in the autumn of 1932, K 2770 started taxiing trials, only to have the left wing collapse. The cause of this was traced back to a design stressing error, which had been unearthed by a bump on the grass airfield. Thus, another sixteen months were to pass before the machine actually took to the air for the first time, in May 1934. Dogged by the now traditional pitch control sensitivity problems, an unreliable engine and a top speed of 165mph at 15,000 feet, nearly 20mph slower than that of the RAF's then standard Hawker Hart day bomber, it is little wonder that the whole project was quietly abandoned. (Westland)

The sole **Fieseler F-3 Wespe**, or Wasp, D-19556, started its life on the drawing board of Alexander Lippisch as his Delta IV. Completed in 1932, the design was aimed at the light aircraft owner market and, as such, incorporated wing folding for garage storage and a towing hook for transit to the airfield. Engine power for the two-seater was provided by twin 75hp Pobjoy Rs, mounted in push-me-pull-you style. As can be seen here, Lippisch, in an attempt to improve take-off performance, had added a small foreplane elevator. Unfortunately, this surface brought the machine's dynamic centre of pressure forward and made the aircraft tail heavy and tricky to fly. It was these handling difficulties that led to the F-3's abandonment in the autumn of 1933, after it killed its pilot during an attempt to land. (Cowin Collection)

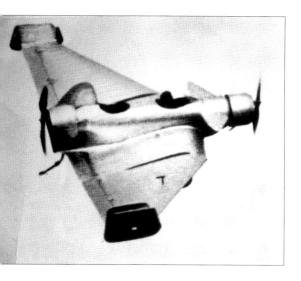

The one-off **Handley Page HP 75 Manx**, H0222, was destined to lead the life of an unwanted and awkward child. Even within the company, its surprisingly extended existence appears to have been more tolerated than encouraged. With its design initiated in April 1936, the Manx first taxied on 29 February 1940, and after an unscheduled hop on 12 September 1942, made it first real flight on June 25th, 1943. From this point on, until quietly abandoned in December 1946, flights and flight time barely got into two figures, totalling 31 and 17 hours, 43 minutes, respectively. Generally considered to have been little more than an Aerodynamics Department toy, the HP 75 was crewed by a pilot and a rear-facing flight test observer. Power was provided by two 140hp DH Gipsy Major IIs, giving the machine a top level speed of 146mph. If the Manx added anything to the fund of tailless aircraft handling knowledge, it remains well hidden. (Handley Page)

The **Northrop N-1M** flew initially on 3 July 1940 and was 'Jack' Northrop's first true flying wing design. Strictly company funded to extend Northrop's knowledge of the subject, the N-1M was a small, low powered machine constructed of wood so as to be readily modifiable. The N-1M, as seen here in its early form, was powered by two 65hp Lycoming O-145s driving pusher propellers and carried anhedral, or downward-canted wingtips. Later fitted with 120hp Franklin radials, the machine had its wingtip straightened out and flew with no significant deterioration in stability. In its later guise, top level speed reached 200mph. All of the early test flying, including the first flight, had been done by Vance Breeze, the famed freelance test pilot, followed by Moye Stephens, doubling as test pilot from his normal role as Company Secretary. At the end of 1941, the sole N-1M, NX-28311 retired with over 200 flights logged. (Northrop)

The second of the **Northrop** flying wings to take to the skies, the **N-9M**, of which four were built, was produced as a just over 1/3 scale flying test bed for the huge four-engined XB-35 bomber ordered by the US Army Air Force in November 1941. First flown on 27 December 1942, with John Myers at the controls, this N-.9M was powered by two 275hp Menasco C6S-4, as were the second and third machines, the fourth N-9M using twin 300hp Franklin O-540-7s to give a top speed of 275mph. Speed, however, was very much secondary to

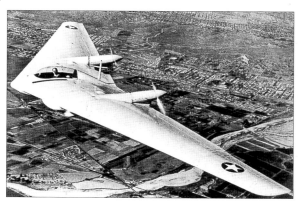

exploring the projected bomber's handling. The vital nature of this work was tragically underlined with the loss of the first N-9M and its pilot, Max Constant, in early 1943. Constant had been carrying out stability checks with an aft centre of gravity when the aircraft crashed The only witness, a farmer, reported that he saw the wings twinkling in the sun as the aircraft fell, indicating either a spin, or a tumble. In what must have been one of its first uses, a hydraulic 'stick pusher' was subsequently fitted to the remaining trio of aircraft to assist the pilot recover from a stalled attitude. (Northrop)

The first of two **Northrop XB-35s**, 42-13603, climbed aloft on its maiden flight on 25 June 1946, with a crew of three headed by Max Stanley. Powered by four 3,000hp Pratt & Whitney R-4360 Wasp Majors driving contra-rotating propellers, the XB-35 had a top level speed of 391mph at 35,000 feet. Its range with a 16,000lb bombload and a 183mph cruising speed was estimated to be 8, 150 miles, a figure never likely to have been verified because of the constant combining gearbox and propeller problems encountered. The P61, incidentally, served not only as a chase plane, but also as a receiver of real time flight test data transmitted from the bomber using a US Navy supplied television link. This must have been one of the earliest examples of securing vital test results that would previously have been lost had the test aircraft crashed. Shown above right is the first of the two **YB-49** jet powered conversions of YB-35s. This machine, 42.10236,

initially flew on 21 October 1947. Powered by six 4,000lb s.t Allison J35-A-15s, the YB-49's top level speed of 493mph at 20,000 feet may have been over 100mph faster than the piston engined XB-35, but the thirst of these early jet engines can be gauged by the greatly reduced warload/range capability of 3,15. miles with a 10,000lb bombload. On 5 June 1948, the secon YB-49 broke up in flight during forward centre of gravity check killing all five crew members. Programme cancellation followe in 1949, resulting, according to a Wright Patterson assessment from insurmountable instability problems. (Northrop)

Above The first of three **De Havilland DH 108s**, TG 283, at Hatfield prior to its 15 May 1946 maiden flight. Produced as a small flying test bed for the DH 106 Comet airliner that was originally designed to be tailless, this first DH 108 was always intended to be the low speed test vehicle and as such made maximum use of existing DH Vampire components, including the whole fuselage. Significantly, Capt. Eric Brown, RN, then commanding the RAE's Aerodynamics Flight flew this machine soon after Geoffrey de Havilland, the younger, had made the first flight. Shortly after going airborne Brown encountered the predictable pitching problem, in his case at low speed and privately summarised the DH 108 as being 'a killer'. Brown's appraisal was to prove all too true, when, on 1 May 1950, TG 283 spun in and crashed, killing Brown's successor, Sqn. Ldr. George Genders. (De Havilland)

Below The second of the **DH 108** trio, TG 308, took to the air initially, again with Geoffrey de Havilland the younger at the control, in June 1946. With a wing sweep increased from 43 to 46 degrees, this second machine, freed of the 322mph indicated limitation of the prototype, besides its normal test flight schedule, was groomed for an attempt on the 100 kilometre, or 62-mile Closed Circuit world air speed record. In the late afternoon of 27 September 1946, with the company's founder's son at the controls, TG 306 departed Hatfield heading south east. A few minutes later, at 7,000 feet in a shallow dive over the Thames estuary, the aircraft disintegrated at around Mach 0.875, or 650mph, killing its pilot. Subsequent investigation showed a rapid build-up of violent pitching forces to be the culprit. The RAE's research findings had not been acted upon. (De Havilland)

Despite the death of Geoffrey de Havilland the younger when the second DH 108 broke up around him, it was decided to press ahead with the completion of the third **DH 108**, VW 120. First flown on 24 July by the company's Grp. Capt. John Cunningham, VW 120 was to be the most aerodynamically refined of the trio, sporting a more shapely nose and canopy contour refinements. Powered by a 3,750lb s.t. DH Goblin 4, this machine was used to establish a new World 100 kilometre, 62-mile, closed circuit air speed record of 605.23mph on 12 April 1948, flown by the company's John Derry. On 15 February 1950, VG 120 joined its ill-starred brethren, killing its RAE pilot, Sqn. Ldr. J. S. R. Muller-Rowland, when it broke up following high speed-induced run-away pitching. (De Havilland)

Right **Armstrong Whitworth's AW 52** started as a twinkle in Chief Designer, John Lloyd's eye towards the end of 1943. Following flight testing with the AW 52G glider, the Ministry of Supply sanctioned the construction of two AW 52 to serve as 3/4-scale flight test machines for a proposed tailless airliner. The first of the pair, TG 363, seen here, took off for its maiden flight on 13 November 1947, followed by TG 368 on 1 September 1948. Incorporating a laminar airfoiled wing and powered by twin 5,000lb s.t. Rolls-Royce Nenes. These expensive machines proved a bitter disappointment, their laminar wings becoming instantly far less efficient the moment a fly struck their leading edges. To compound matters, the lack of adequate tail moment arm damping produced pitch axis control problems at high speed, leading to the imposition of a 288mph indicated limitation. (Ministry of Supply/Crown Copyright)

Above The sole **EKW N 20 Aiguillon**, designed and developed by the Swiss Federal Aircraft Factory, was an attempt to provide the Swiss Air Force with a potent, home-grown, advanced single-seat jet-powered fighter bomber. Initiated in 1947, the low speed handling had been verified by flight testing a 3/5-scale glider in 1948, followed by higher speed testing of the same scale, but powered EKW Arbalete from November 1951. To fly the N 20 needed an extremely innovative, reheated turbofan engine, latterly built around an Armstrong Siddeley Mamba, as its core gas generator. This engine proved inadequate and the N 20 project was scrapped after one short hop on 8 April 1952.

ARMSTRONG WHITWORTH E9/44
(PROTOTYPE)
NENE
DECEMBER 1946

The Jet, The War and Big Problems, 1939–1945

The jet engine took a long time in coming and when it did, as often happens, with technology, it transpired that a number of people had been working on the same basic idea in parallel. The first studies undertaken by Dr A. A. Griffith, then with the Royal Aircraft Establishment, emerged in 1926 and were for a turbine-driven propeller system, or turboprop. By the mid-1930s a number of teams, including two in Germany, one in Britain and one in Sweden were all working to develop a pure hot-gas expelling turbine, or turbojet. Significantly, while Flt. Lt., later Air Commodore Sir Frank Whittle in Britain and Hans von Ohain of Heinkel in Germany were both producing turbojets with centrifugal compressors, a line of development that was ultimately to give way to the straight through, or axial turbojet, both Maxi Adolf Mueller of Junkers in Germany and A.J. Lysholm, with the help of Botors in Sweden, had already seen the low frontal area advantage of the axial unit; although Lysholm's efforts were later to be abandoned. The winner in the first phase of the race to produce a practical airworthy turbojet, was the Heinkel team, beating the British by just under 21 months. However, the ultimate victor's laurels must go to the British, who after a desultory start, came from behind on the back of superior metallurgy and product engineering. Somewhat surprisingly, the Americans, after a promising, if belated, 1940 start with a Lockheed axial turbojet study, along with Northrop's huge turboprop, tended to fall into line behind British gas turbine technology initially by buying it in directly, followed by much licence-building of British engines, a practice that would continue into the early 1950s. Overall, however, the real impetus to jet engine development, even in simple quantitative terms was not to emerge until the last year of World War II, real qualitative progress having to wait a further few years, spurred on by the Cold War.

With the shadow of war came the inevitable boost to aircraft manufacture. Just when the upswing got underway depended, more or less, on the prescience of individual governments or even industries. Certainly, Germany provided the trigger with its massive re-armament programme commenced in late 1933, the Luftwaffe in the forefront. France and Britain joined the scramble by the close of 1936 and by 1939 were dragging the US aircraft producing sector in by default, as they realised they needed more machines than they had the capacity to produce. This buying panic even saw Britain attempting to buy Italian light bombers at one point, the deal being scuppered when the Italian Dictator, Mussolini, formed the Axis Pact with Hitler in mid-1940. Over the next few years, aircraft production in the US, Russia, Germany and Britain was to reach astronomical heights: 33,000-plus Messerschmitt Bf 109s, 22,800 Spitfire/Seafires, along with well in excess of 13,000 Curtiss P-40 Warhawks and around 15,000 each of Republic's P-47 Thunderbolt and North American's P-51 Mustang - and these were only some of the fighters!

As mentioned earlier, major wars may boost aircraft and aero-engine building enormously, but usually to the detriment of aeronautical research and innovation. What happens to research is that effort tends to get switched from exploring the more esoteric to practical problem solving. Thus, aerodynamicists previously engaged in studying aspects of high speed flight are switched to finding a cure for progressive elevator heaviness being experienced with Spitfires in high speed dives. Aircraft design teams become equally preoccupied with the next Mk., or even a problem with an existing Mk., rather than the next design. Aircraft designers at the beginning of World War II had certain traits in common. Initially, most had cut their design 'teeth' as junior designers during World War I, or immediately after. This period and well into the 1930s saw aviation design in a state of constant renewal. Thus, anyone growing into the job during these years was exposed to much 'on the job training', coupled to what can best be termed design practice influences. This is best

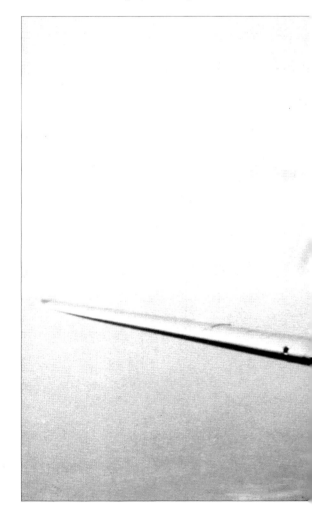

illustrated by comparison of R. J. Mitchell, who led the design of the Supermarine Spitfire and Sidney, later Sir Sidney, Camm, creator of the Hawker Hurricane. Mitchell's background had been in the design of flying boats and racing floatplanes, both of which traditionally favoured the use of metal construction and the employment of thin, high speed airfoil wing section for the racers. Both of these aspects came to the fore in Mitchell's innovative Spitfire, whereas Camm's background in robust wooden biplane structures shows through in the more conservatively constructed Hurricane and even more so in its successor, the very powerful Hawker Typhoon, whose disdain for high speed airfoils was to bring a spate of fatalities in the wake of the Typhoon's rushed service introduction. Camm, even according to colleague biographers, was never predisposed towards the aerodynamics of design, he was a structures man, and a very good one too.

The one big problem facing the airframe designers of this period was that, collectively, few if any understood the ramifications of what little work had been published from the early 1930s onwards concerning flight into the high speed compressibility region, where sonic shockwaves did not simply produce sudden, huge jumps in overall aerodynamic drag, but simultaneously altered an aircraft's handling in a dramatic and dangerous fashion. This at a time when the larger aero-engine builders were just stepping up to produce a new breed of 2,000hp power units. The combination of aircraft designers' attempts to squeeze the maximum performance out of the existing machines by 'cleaning them up', while fitting ever more powerful engines, was by late 1941-early 1942, to ensure that a significant number of young fighter pilots met a premature death, not at the hands of an enemy, but because of the then little understood effect of diving into the region of compressibility, where their machines became mysteriously uncontrollable. Most of these young men were to die by overstressing their aircraft in their efforts to recover control.

Vought-Sikorsky's XF4U-1 prototype of the F4U Corsair, seen here on 4 May 1941, nearly a year into its extended flight testing. Powered by a 1,850hp Pratt & Whitney XR2800-4 with its monumental, 16-ft diameter propeller, the Corsair, along with the Focke-Wulf FW 190 and Hawker Typhoon, was to usher in the new breed of 2,000hp engines. It was these extremely powerful engines attached to relatively light airframes that were to drag most combat aircraft designers unwittingly into their first confrontation with flight in the compressibility zone and new dangers. (US Navy)

This wartime British official photograph of a **Hawker Typhoon Ib** in frontal aspect is captioned 'A Typhoon shows its teeth'. From the black and white 'invasion' stripes, it is evident that this picture was taken in, or after, early June 1944. The telltale stripes also highlight the inordinately thick airfoil section of this 2,000hp Napier Sabre-powered fighter wing. A number lost their tail units, almost inevitably with fatal results, as a result of being dived into the compressibility zone, which in the Typhoon's case was a little below Mach 0.7. Rushed into service in an attempt to counter the Focke-Wulf FW 190 threat, this propensity to lose its tail led, in the short term, to the Typhoon's role being changed from that of interceptor to fighter bomber, pending the arrival of its thin wing-sectioned successor, the Hawker Tempest. The Tempest's thin elliptical wing made it look quite like the Spitfire. Incidentally, while the Typhoon might have been 'worst case', it was certainly not alone. Other 'tail shedders' included the Focke-Wulf FW 190 and Lockheed's P-38 Lightning.
(British official Crown Copyright)

The **Supermarine Spitfire PR XI** was used by the RAE, along with Republic's P-47 Thunderbolt and North American's P-51 Mustang, to carry out comparative tests into the high speed handling of these machines in late 1943-1944. At this time, the only research route was to 'go fly it' in a real aircraft as no reliable wind tunnel data on flight behaviour between Mach 0.85 and Mach 1.25 could be obtained until the advent of

the slotted high speed tunnels at the beginning of the 1950s. As it transpired, the limiting speeds of the test trio varied considerably, the thin-winged Spitfire's being Mach 0.9, that of the P-51 being Mach 0.81 and that for the P-47, a meagre Mach 0.73. Actual aircraft handling varied even more markedly, with the Spitfire proving the most docile, followed relatively closely by the P-51, while the P-47 came a poor third. (Vickers)

The sole **Heinkel He 178**, seen here in a 'still' from Heinkels own film record of the taxiing trials. Secrecy of both the military and commercial variety surrounded this machine, the first aircraft anywhere in the world to be entirely propelled by turbojet. First flown officially on 27 August 1939, the machine had, in fact, made a short airborne hop three days previously. Built as a flying test bed for the 1,100lb s.t. Heinkel HeS 3B with its centrifugal compressor, the He 178's initial flight testing was done with the landing gear locked down and temporary fairings over the wheel wells. That development went relatively well can be gauged from the fact that the He 178 was demonstrated before top German Air Ministry officials three months later. Top level speed attained by the He 178 was cited at 435mph. (Cowin Collection)

The **Caproni-Campini N.1** was, chronologically, the world' second jet aircraft to fly, this feat taking place at Milan on 27 August 1940, one year and three days after the He 178's maiden flight. On paper, the N.1's propulsion system embodied several very advanced concepts, including an afterburning, high by-pass turbofan. What it turned out to be was a 'Mickey Mouse' compound contraption of a 900hp Isotta-Fraschini driving a ducted fan, with a fuel-guzzling afterburning combustor ring thrown in. The overall result of this means of propulsion can be determined from the machine's top level speed of 205mph at 9,800 feet, increased by a mere 28mph at the same altitude with afterburner working. Some indication of fuel consumption can be gleaned from the fact that the machine had to alight at Pisa for fuel while making a 169-mile cross-country flight between Milan and Rome. Testing of the N.1 ceased in the spring of 1941. (Italian Air Ministry)

The product of Alexander Lippisch's fertile brain, the rocket powered **Messerschmitt Me 1638-1a Komet**, seen here at the Peenemunde-West flight test centre, was not only the world's first rocket-powered fighter to be deployed operationally, it was also the first ever tailless fighter to enter service. First flown unpowered during the spring of 1941 and with power a few months later. The first operational deployment of this 660-3,300lb variable thrust BMW 109-510 powered machine took place on 16 August 1944, when Komets of JG 400 intercepted Boeing B-17s near the Leuna oil refinery. The Komet's twin 30mm MK. 108 cannons may have been prone to stoppages, but this was the least of the machine's problems. Using highly volatile liquid fuels to provide a high specific thrust, these same unstable propellants frequently exploded when jarred, such as in landing. As the number of overall 'kills' attributed to the Me 163 were 7, plus 2 probables, it is clear that kill-to-loss ratio for this fighter was all wrong. They may have frightened US bomber crews, but, they did not kill many. The Komet also had a relatively low threshold of Mach 0.82 to compressibility, which invariably forced the aircraft into a dive. (Cowin Collection)

Gloster's G.40, more popularly known by its Air Ministry Specification, E.28/39, like the earlier Heinkel He 178, was produced purely as a flight test bed for British turbojet development. The G.40, W 4041/G, Britain's first pure turbojet powered aircraft first flew on 15 May 1941, followed by the first flight of W 4046IG a year and nine months later, on 1 March 1943. Both aircraft were fitted with various Frank Whittle-designed engines, ranging from the earliest 850lb s.t. W.1 to the later 1,526lb s.t. Rolls-Royce W.2B123 and 1,700lb s. t. Power Jets W.21500. Top level speed reached by the short-lived second prototype is cited at 466mph, this machine crashing on 30 July 1943, after spinning inverted from 37,000 feet. The pilot, Sqn. Ldr. Douglas Davie, baled out safely.
(Gloster Aircraft)

The **Messerschmitt Me 262A-1a**, powered by two 1,980lb s.t. Junkers Jurno 0048s, first saw action against US daylight bombers on 3 October 1944. The Me 262 ultimately proved to be a far more effective fighter than the Me 163. Not only did the Me 262 have a higher critical speed than the Me 163, Mach 0.86 compared with the latter's Mach 0.82, it also outgunned, out-ranged and generally handled better than the Komet.

An interesting aspect of the Me 262 design was its use of a modest degree of sweep-back to its wings, something German aerodynamicists had discovered would delay the onset of compressibility effects in 1939. Clearly, the Messerschmitt team were actually paying heed to this research, a fact that explains why with less power, the Me 262A's top level speed of 536mph at 22,880 feet, compared very favourably with the rival Gloster Meteor F I's 410mph at its optimum altitude of 30,000 feet. The Me 262A-1a's armament comprised four 30mm MK. 108, while later versions carried a mix of two 30mm, plus four 20mm cannons in the nose. There were just over 100 Me 262s losses in combat, the vast majority of which were the result of their pilots either slowing down to make a more accurate attack, or being caught on approach to land. (Cowin Collection)

America's first jet, the **Bell P-59 Airacomet** was ordered into development on 30 September 1941, with the first of two prototype XP-59As making its maiden flight a year and a day later, on 1 October 1942. A total of 65 Bell P-59s were to be built in all, comprising the two XP-59As, 13 development YP-59As and 50 production P-59As. Initially powered by a pair of 1,300lb s.t. General Electric 1A turbojets, an Americanised version of the Power Jets W.2B, the P-59As used the 1,650lb

s.t. General Electric I-16, later known as the J31. Top level speed was an unremarkable 409mph at 35,000 feet and this, coupled with the P59A's generally disappointing performance when tested against the P-38 and P-47 in December 1943, led to it being declared unfit for combat and relegation to jet familiarisation and fighter training duties. Armament varied, but later models carried one 37mm cannon, plus three .5 inch machine guns. Normal range was 240 miles. (Bell)

Below The **Gloster G.41**, DG 204/G was the third of eight prototypes of what were to become the Meteor. DG 204/G was the only one to be fitted with two 1,800lb s.t. Metropolitan Vickers F2 axial turbojets originating from the work of Dr A.A. Griffith at the RAE. Readily distinguishable from the other prototypes by its underslung engine nacelles, DG 204/G first took to the air on 13 November 1943, a little over eight months after that of the first G.41, a DH Goblin-powered machine, on 5 March 1943. DG 204/G's brief flying career ended catastrophically on 1 April 1944, when it was lost following an in-flight engine disintegration, fatally injuring its pilot Sqn. Ldr. Douglas Davie. (Power Jets Ltd/Crown Copyright)

This **Gloster Meteor 1**, EE 227, was to become the world's first turboprop aircraft to fly when, on 30 September 1945, Gloster's Eric Greenwood was to take it aloft on the power of two 750eshp and 1,000lb s.t. Rolls-Royce Trents. Later, when fitted with smaller diameter propellers, these figures shifted to

350eshp and 1,400lb s.t. The Trent was a Derwent 11 modified to take a forward drive shaft, a reduction gearbox and a five-bladed propeller. While the Trent was not a success in itself, its development and flight testing contributed materially to the early emergence of its successor, the Rolls-Royce Dart. (Rolls-Royce)

Right The vertically launched, rocket powered **Bachen Ba 349A** represented the ultimate in German World War II manned local, or point air defence capability. Armed with twenty four 73mm rocket projectiles in its nose, the Ba 349A's single 3,748lb Waiter HWK 509A-2 liquid fuel rocket was

augmented for launching with two 2,756lb solid fuel jettison-able boosters. Top level speed with the nose fairing ejected ready for firing, as seen here, was around 400mph during the attack phase, after which speed decayed to 155mph and it was here that pilot/airframe separation took place, both then descending by parachute. From launch to 40,000 feet and back down to separation took less than 2 minutes! First flown under tow from a Heinkel He III in October 1944, the Ba 349's general handling was considered admirable, but subsequent powered testing led to at least one pilot fatality. (Cowin Collection)

The salient features of the **Miles M.52** transonic research aircraft can be determined from this view of one of the makers' stainless steel scale models used for wind tunnel testing. The development of this potentially pivotal project was launched in November 1943 to Ministry of Supply Specification E.24143, the project being cancelled in February 1946. As an aircraft, the M.52 embodied a number of innovative features, along with some that were forced upon the designers by the technological limitations of the time. Among the novelties was the use of an all flying, or slab, tailplane. Another feature of interest was the unswept, thin, bi-convex airfoil wing, later to appear on Bell's XS-1, later X-1, Douglas's X-3 and Lockheed's F-104 Starfighter. Some of the impositions brought about the use of a an extremely confining cockpit-cum-escape capsule, foreshadowing that used on the Bell X-2. Besides providing the pilots with poor forward visibility, there is a very real question as to whether the capsule would have cleared the aircraft cleanly in the case of a high speed emergency. The fuselage-mounted, narrow track landing gear, necessitated by the thin wing, was

another item most pilots would have preferred to do without. Power for the M.52 was to have been provided by a 2,000lb s.t. Whittle W.21700, boosted to 3,175lb s.t. with afterburning; whether this would have provided sufficient impulse to allow the aircraft to approach the critical Mach No. of 1.5 at 30,000 feet, or 1,002mph, seems doubtful, explaining why Miles were already planning a 6,500lb s.t. Rolls-Royce A.J. 65, later Avon, powered version. This raises another conundrum – did the 2,500lb overload fuel capacity of the M.52 allow a conventional take-off, climb to around 40,000 feet, a shallow reheat-power dive and retrieval to base? The one fact that does emerge is that on 9 October 1948, a joint Vickers-RAE rocket-powered 3/10th-scale fully instrumented model of the M.52 was launched from a DH Mosquito flying at 35,500 feet and achieved Mach 1.38, or 911mph in straight and level flight. This event proved that Miles had, at least, got their aerodynamics right. (Miles Aircraft)

Prototypes in Profusion, 1947–1964

This period between the beginning of the Cold War and American involvement in South East Asia, brought about a vast number of wildly different prototypes. By this time the US was out in front in almost every area of aviation/aerospace activity, followed not too distantly by the Soviets. Britain was not too far behind the US in terms of airframe technology and ahead when it came to engine development. Sadly, this period saw Britain's resolve and assets frittered away, whereas France picked itself up and, by the early 1960s, was showing Britain the way in the fighter aircraft markets of the world. It is worth recalling that the English Electric/BAC Lightning was Britain's main export hope at the start of the 1960s, while the French hoped for similar success with their Dassault Mirage III. By 1970 Lightning production was complete, including its total export order book of 46 aircraft, while Dassault were just getting their multi-thousand Mirage III and V export programme underway. The lesson that the British should have learned was that the world's smaller air forces did not have the operational needs of the RAF, nor could they afford to buy and maintain a complex, twin-engined machine.

Aviation technology during this period was shaped by events both within and beyond its immediate application. One example of outside influences shaping development is the rise and fall of the rapid-reaction rocket-cum-jet local defence interceptor. Information on aircraft rocket development and associated rapid-reaction air defence thinking had flowed out

of Germany in the months following the end of World War II. Leading fighter designers everywhere then turned their attention to employing the rocket to thrust their designs skywards at unprecedented rates of climb, from whence their machines switched over to the jet engine for the return flight. The US, France and Britain all devoted considerable study to such aircraft, only to realise that the rocket engines performed even more spectacularly when fitted into surface-to-air missiles. These missiles rendered the high speed, high altitude bomber threat redundant and removed the need for fast-reaction interceptors. Steady improvements in metallurgy, machining and materials brought giant strides in jet engine performance, while the introduction of solid-state and other reliability-enhancing developments in electronics were reflected in numerous advances, ranging from better flight controls to radio and navigational aids. The one cloud on the horizon for the specialists came in the form of the US Secretary of Defense, Robert McNamara, part of the 1960 John F. Kennedy team, and an interservice equipment commonality policy. By 1963 the McDonnell F-4 Phantom II, designed for the US Navy in the late 1950s as a dedicated all-weather interceptor, was being deployed by the US Navy, the US Marines and the USAF not just as an interceptor, but as a bomb-hauling tactical fighter too. The day of the overly specialised combat design was over. Cost effectiveness was the slogan, even if it led to costly debacles, such as the early years of the General Dynamics/Grumman F-111/F-111B.

Below left This 1949 wind tunnel model of what was to become the **English Electric P.1A** of 1954 provides an insight into the vital part the wind tunnel plays in the transition from drawing board to flyable prototype. While recognisable as a precursor of the RAF's Mach 2 Lightning, the tail unit configuration, along with the low mounted wings, caused severe pitch-up forces at transonic speeds. An item of possible interest to trainspotters is the uncanny resemblance of this model's windscreen to that of the Deltic locomotive built for British Rail by another English Electric Division. (Hugh W. Cowin)

Top **Lockheed P-80A**, 44.85214, was the first of two P-80As to flight test experimental ramjet during the early post-World War II years. Pioneered by the Frenchman, Rene Leduc, who started his work on ramjets in 1929, the concept involves a suitably shaped combustor tube with one or more fuel/air mixing injector rings mounted upstream of an igniter ring or rings, thus providing an engine with no moving parts. The one snag to this system was that is required a certain minimum airflow through it to initiate and sustain ignition. After the P-80A flight trials that extended from March 1947 into early 1949, the ramjet fell from favour as an aircraft speed booster except in France. The ramjet did, however, find a home, being employed as cruise sustaining propulsion on missiles using booster rockets for launch. As seen here, 44.85214 has just started up its two 30 inch Marquart C39.10B wingtip mounted ramjets. (US Air Force)

Above right In the years immediately after World War II, no national aviation industry was more innovative and daring than the French, as shown by such as **Aerocentre's NC 1071**. Claimed at the time to be aimed at providing an aircraft carrier going jet trainer, the unconventional NC 1071 was powered by two 4,850lb s.t. Rolls-Royce Nenes, giving this three seater a top level speed of 493mph at 19,685 feet. First flown on 12 October 1948, one of this heavyweight's major problems would be finding an aircraft carrier large enough to accept it, particularly when the US had yet to launch the first of its super carriers. Whatever it was, the NC 1071 goes down in the records as being France's first twin jet. (GIFAS)

Lt. Cdr. Michael J. 'Mike' Lithgow, Chief Test Pilot for Vickers Armstrong's Supermarine company standing beside the sole Supermarine 510, VV 106, which he demonstrated at the September 1949 SBAC Farnborough Air Show. A former Royal Navy Fleet Air Arm pilot, Lithgow's association with Supermarine started in 1944, when he was seconded to the company to assist Jeffrey Quill in Spitfire/Seafire development flying. After the war, Quill persuaded Lithgow to join the firm,

where he succeeded Quill as Chief Test Pilot in 1947. During the late 1940s and early 1950s, 'Mike' Lithgow had overall flight development responsibility for the string of Supermarine designs that sired the RAF's Swift and the Royal Navy's Scimitar.

Tragically, Lt. Cdr. Lithgow, along with his co-pilot 'Dickie' Rymer and three flight test engineers were to lose their lives in the prototype BAC One-Eleven's 'deep stall' crash of 22 October 1963. Shown above is the sole **Supermarine 510**, VV 106, which began the evolution of the Attacker and the Swift. First flown on 29 December 1948, with Lithgow at the controls, he was also flying the 510, by now equipped with arrester hook, when it became the first fully swept-winged aircraft to land aboard a carrier, during trials with HMS *Illustrious* on 8 November 1950. (Vickers)

Destined to become the world's first purely jet powered transport, this **Vickers Viking** had originally been delivered to the Ministry of Supply with the military serials VX 856 as a high altitude test bed for new types of engines. Following a switch to civil registration, G-AJPH, the machine initially flew powered by its two 5,000lb s.t. Rolls-Royce Nenes on 6 April 1948. Converted back to its original Bristol Hercules-engined form, G-AJPH ended its flying career serving with the British independent Eagle Aviation. (Vickers)

McDonnell's diminutive **XF-85 Goblin** was to be the last attempt of the twentieth century to produce a dedicated parasite fighter. Work on the XF-85 started during the latter half of 1944 to meet a USAAF need for a fighter that could be carried and deployed from their B-29, B-35 and B-36 long-range bombers in order to protect them. Starting with a small, relatively conventional design, the tiny single seater evolved into its final, quite radical shape by mid-1945, under pressure to make it fully stowable within the bomber's fuselage. First flown

free of the trapeze-equipped Boeing B-29 mothership on 23 August 1948, the two XF-85s, 46.523 and 46.524 proved far too sensitive in their handling to permit routine launch and recovery, flight testing being abandoned in April 1949. after a meagre 2 hours, 19 minutes aloft. Powered by a 3,000lb s.t. Westinghouse J34-W-7, the four .5 inch gunned XF-85's top level speed was never established. Combat endurance was estimated at 30 minutes. (McDonnell Aircraft)

Convair's sole **XF-92A**, 46.682, the world's first jet powered delta winged aircraft, seen here at Muroc Dry Lake with its Convair Project Pilot, Ellis D. 'Sam' Shannon. Powered by a 4,600lb s.t. Allison J33-A-21, Shannon took the XF-92 aloft for an initial hop on 11 June 1948 and also carried out the first full flight three months later on 18 September, by which time the 5,200lb s.t. J33-A-23 had been fitted. Already relegated to the role of delta wing research, having lost the fighter competition to Republic's mixed power XF-91, the XF-92A proved a disappointment. Designed under the tutorial eyes of Alexander Lippisch, the XF-92A was never able to exceed the speed of sound in level flight, although 'Chuck' Yeager is reported to have once pushed the XF-92 to Mach 1.1 in a dive. As with many

unwanted military prototypes, the XF-92A was ultimately handed over to the NACA, who equipped it with an 8,500lb s.t. reheated J33-A-29 in May 1951, but even with this larger engine, top level speed remained at around Mach 0.9 in high speed handling trials with the machine between April and October 1953 (Convair)

Illuminated by the flame of its 2,755lb SEPR 251 rocket, the **Sud Ouest S.O. 6025 Espadon** prepares to roll for take-off. First flown on 28 December 1949, the S.O. 6025 was the third of four Espadons, including the original S.0. 6020 fighter reconnaissance prototype. Powered by a 5,000lb s.t. Rolls-Royce Nene, the first Espadon had made its maiden flight on 12 November 1948. Although not selected to go forward into production, the four Espadons served in a research capacity, particularly to test various performance-enhancing auxiliary rocket engines that pushed the aircraft's top sea level speed to 621mph, or took the machine to 33,000 feet in 9 minutes. One basic feature of the Espadon's design was its use of an F-16 style ventral intake for its Nene. (GIFAS)

Sir Sydney Camm, as a young man of twenty two pictured here in 1915 at a Syfleet, Surrey aeromodelling meet. Camm had become Secretary of the Windsor Model Aeroplane Club in April 1912, at a time when such clubs also tried their hand at designing man-carrying aircraft. This provided Camm with the opportunity to take part in the creation of two manned gliders and a 20hp light aircraft prior to the outbreak of World War I. At this time, Camm joined Martinsydes, one of the Brooklands-based aircraft producers. Camm spent the

war years between honing his woodworking skills and aeronautical journalism, prior to joining his chief, G. H Handasyde, in late 1921. Here he helped draw up the design of a glider for the famed Itford Hill, Sussex, trials. In 1923, Sidney Camm was to join the Hawker Engineering Company's drawing office, where he flourished, becoming Chief Designer in 1925 and from where he was to lead the teams that produced the Hawker Hart, Fury, Hurricane and Hunter. It is generally

acknowledged that in later years Sir Sydney viewed aerodynamics and those that practised the art as somewhat peripheral to the main business of aircraft building. (British Aerospace)

Hawker's P.1052 was a derivative of the company's first jet, their unswept P.1040 of late 1944 that was to become the Seahawk. With the availability of captured German data on swept wings, the P.1052 represented the first in a series of faltering steps that was to see the company lose pride of place as a producer of outstanding fighters. Powered by a 5,000lb s.t. Rolls-Royce Nene and built to Specification E.38146, the P.1052's task was researching the aerodynamics of a Mach 0.86 limited, 35 degree swept wing of 10 per cent thickness to chord ratio. Useful as this information may have been in late 1945 or 1946, by the time the P.1052's first flight took place on 19 November 1948, there is little doubt that the need for such data had long past. Indeed by this time, the fully swept Mig-15, North American F-86 Sabre, Boeing B-47 Stratojet and SAAB J29 were all in, or about to enter, production. (Hawker Aircraft)

Converted from the second P.1052, VX 279, the sole **Hawker P.1081** had started life as an aspirant fighter design for the Royal Australian Air Force and again represented a fairly minimalist approach when set against its contemporaries, such as the North American F-86 Sabre, which won the Australian order. Still using the forward fuselage of the P.1040 Seahawk, the P.1081 abandoned the split, or bifurcated jet exhaust pipes in favour of a straight-through jet pipe taken from a

Supermarine Attacker, The major change to the P.1081 were the all-new, fully swept fin and tail surfaces. Powered with the same 5,000lb s.t. Nene as its forebear, the P.1081 first took to the air on 19 June 1950. The top level speed of VX 279 was Mach 0.89 at 36,000 feet, or 588mph, 14mph faster than the P.1052. VX 279 crashed, cause unknown, on 3 April 1951, killing Hawker's Chief Test Pilot, Sqn. Ldr. T .S. 'Wimpy' Wade. (Hawker Aircraft)

Avro 707, VX 784, the first of five delta-winged 707s built as roughly 1/3rd-scale flight test machines for Avro's forthcoming Vulcan. VX 784, was first flown on 4 September 1949, powered by a 3,500lb s.t. Rolls-Royce Derwent 5 and was meant to test low speed Vulcan handling. Unfortunately, the aircraft had hardly entered flight testing, when, on 30 September, it crashed following a loss of control, killing Avro's Deputy Chief Test Pilot, E .S. Esler. This loss set the 707 research programme back by almost a year, with the first flight of the second low speed aircraft, 707B, VX 790, not taking place until 6 September 1950, thanks to the need to fit the machine with ejector seat and other modifications. (Avro)

Below The third of the 707 quintet was WD 280, first of the two **707As**, the variant cleared for exploring the higher speed region of the Vulcan's flight envelope. Employing a wing and wing root engine air intake identical to that of the forthcoming bomber, the two 707As made several vital contributions in hastening Vulcan development, along with improving its subsequent handling characteristics. A part of this involved stripping out WD 280's original flight controls and replacing them with a system of fully powered, irreversible, hydraulically actuated pitch and roll controls. The 707As did a surprisingly manful job when you consider that their 3,600lb s.t. Rolls-Royce Derwent 8s produced only 100lb s.t. more than the low speed first prototype's power output, despite a jump of 14 per cent in the 707A's all-up-weight. The fifth and final member of the family was the sole 707C. a side-by-side two seater, later to become Britain's first fly-by-wire aircraft. (Avro)

Above right The **Avro Ashton** was one of the largest aircraft to be produced for pure research. Largely unsung, the high altitude flight testing of engines and equipment carried out by these aircraft, with their unprecedented space in which to house the necessary complement of flight test observers and their instruments, contributed materially in maintaining Britain in the forefront of aero-engine development well into the 1960s. First flown on 1 September 1950, the sole Mk. 1 was followed by a single Mk. 2, three Mk. 3s and a final, single Mk. 4, the latter making its first flight on 18 November 1952. All six employed four 5,000lb s.t. Rolls-Royce Nenes as their basic propulsion, with additional test engines being carried as required. Seen here lifting off from Filton is WB 493, the second of the three Mk. 3s, piloted by Bristol Siddeley Engines' Chief

est Pilot, Wg. Cdr. Walter Gibbs. Photographed on 2 February 955, the machine carries two reheated Bristol Siddeley Olympus outboard of the Nenes. (Bristol Siddeley)

elow The sole **Boulton Paul P.111**, VT 935 was contracted in November 1946 under Specification E.27146 to research delta wing handling at high speed and first flew some three years, nine months later, on 6 October 1950. The P.111's sole stablemate, the P.120, VT 951 employed the same basic wing and fuselage, but carried a much modified fin and rudder, to which had been added an all-flying, or slab tailplane mounted twothirds up the fin. The P.120 first went aloft early in August 1952. Quite what these machines were envisaged to achieve with the relatively modest 5,100lb s.t of their single Rolls-Royce Nenes begs a host of questions. The highest speed known to have been reached by the P.111 in level flight was Mach 0.935 at 5,000 feet, or 622mph, during 1953 trials. (Boulton Paul)

Bottom left The short-lived **Boulton Paul P.120**, first flown on 6 August 1952, ended spectacularly a little over three weeks later, on the 29th. The highest speed known to have been reached by the P.120 was Mach 0.68 at 4,000 feet, or 518mph, moments before it lost its left -side elevon. Fortunately, Boulton Paul's Chief Test Pilot, A.E. 'Ben' Gunn ejected successfully, going on to end his career in airport management. (Boulton Paul)

The sole **Fairey FD 1**, VX 350 seen at rest with wing leading edge slots open. First flown by Fairey's Grp. Capt. R.G. Slade on 12 March 1951, he had initiated taxi tests ten months earlier on 12 May 1950. However, so violent were the pitching moments as the machine gathered speed that Gordon Slade

insisted that the porpoising be remedied before he would fly it. The remedy came in the shape of the small, fixed tailplane, which restricted the machine's maximum speed to below 345mph, demolishing all thought of reaching the estimated 628mph at 10,000 feet. Above is a rare air-to-air view of VX 350. The cylindrical housing projecting rearwards below the jet pipe is for the braking parachute. (Fairey Aviation)

Overleaf **Bell's X-5** caught against something closely resembling a lunar landscape that turns out to be an area just north of Edwards AFB. Based on the Messerschmitt P.1101 interceptor that had a three-position, variable sweep angled wing that required setting before each flight. Bell took the concept on a stage, providing an in-flight adjustable sweep

range from 20 to 60 degrees, compared with the P.1101's 35 to 45 degree movement. Two X-5s were built for the US Air Force, 50.1838 and 50.1839, the type's first flight being made on 20 June 1951. The second machine was destroyed when it spun in on 14 October 1953, fatally injuring Major Raymond Popson. Above is a revealing ground view of the surviving X-5, 50.1838. The inherent flexibility of the underslung engine mounting was one emphasised by Bell as permitting real choice of engine fit when they came to push the US Air Force to consider buying a fighter development of the X-5. The US Air Force rejection of this proposal was based on the overall small size of the X-5. The X-5''s final flight was made on 25 October 1955, by no less a future luminary than Neil Armstrong. (Bell)

Bottom The sole **Handley Page HP 88**, VX 330, was designed and constructed to flight test the more radical aerodynamic features of the company's forthcoming Victor bomber. Sadly, the HP 88's appearance was so delayed that it almost overtaken by the real thing, much of which had already been redesigned anyway. Very much a hybrid, with a specially supplied fuselage from Supermarine, coupled to wings and tail unit designed by Handley Page, sub-contracted for assembly by General Aircraft but delayed due to that company's acquisition by Blackburn who were in charge of the HP 88's overall completion. It flew for the first time on 21 June 1951. Powered by a 5,000lb s.t. Rolls-Royce Nene 2, the HP 88 had displayed from the outset undue control sensitivity in the pitching axis. In an attempt to cure the problem, VX 330 had just been modified to take a RAE devised 'plumb bob' pitch control damper when it was handed over to Handley Page for the high speed handling phase. Immediately after this, on 26 August 1951, while flying a high speed, low level run at 300 feet above Stansted Airfield's runway, the HP 88 suffered structural failure at 547mph, killing Handley Page's Douglas J. Broomfield. The crash cause was attributed to the inclusion of the 'plum bob', ironically, fitted to a tailplane long since redesigned for the Victor. (Blackburn)

Opposite, top The sole **Short SB.5**, WG 768, seen in its final form, with wings swept at 69 degrees and a low set tailplane. Built specifically as a low speed research vehicle to test the aerodynamics and handling of English Electric's P.1A prototype for the Lightning, the S8.5 was to prove highly successful. First flown on 2 December 1952, just short of twenty one months ahead of the P.1A., The SB.5 was initially powered by 3.600lb s.t. Rolls-Royce Derwent, but when ultimately re-configured as shown in 1957, was refitted with a 5,000lb s.t. Bristol Orpheus. Initially flown with a 50 degree wing sweep and a delta planform tailplane atop the fin and rudder, the SB.5 had by January 1954 been reconfigured to have a 60 degree wing sweep, plus low set tailplane as in the P.1A. In this form, the machine was to provide English Electric's chief Test Pilot Wg. Cdr. Roland Beamont 22 opportunities to experience the P.1A's low speed handling prior to its early August 1954 maiden flight. (Shorts)

Aimed at providing a rapid interception capability against high speed, high altitude threats, the prototype **Sud Ouest S.O. 9000 Trident** was first flown on 2 March 1953. The main propulsion consisted of a three-barrelled SEPR 48 rocket engine providing a total thrust of 8,265lb, backed by two 880lb s.t. Turbomeca Marbore IIs, soon found inadequate for the task and replaced by two 1,640lb s.t. Armstrong Siddeley Vipers. The Trident's maximum level speed of Mach 1.6 at 36,000 feet and above, or 1,056mph, could only be maintained for 4 minutes 30 seconds. A second example was destroyed during its initial flight in September 1953. (GIFAS)

First flown on 19 July 1955, the **Sud Ouest S.O. 9050 Trident II** is seen here cruising on the power of its two 3,307lb s.t. Turbomeca Gazibo wingtip-mounted turbojets. Rocket power still provided the main propulsion for interception but was now provided by a twin-barrel SEPR 631 giving a total thrust of 6,614lb. This shift in the balance of installed power between the Trident and Trident II was clearly targeted at extending the machine's radius of action by allowing the machine to rely more on its upgraded turbojets. The Trident II's initial climb rate of 19,685 feet per minute and high altitude capability were shown on 2 May 1958, when it set a new absolute height record of 79,452 feet. Seen here carrying a mock-up of an air-to-air missile beneath its fuselage, one of the three Trident IIs was lost on 21 May 1957 as a result of an in-flight explosion of the volatile liquid rocket fuel. This notwithstanding, neither

America's Republic XF-91, or Britain's Saunders-Roe S.R. 53 mixed power interceptors ever achieved the stage of development reached by the Trident II. (GIFAS)

The intriguing **Convair XF2Y-1 Seadart** jet-powered hydro-skied interceptor reflected the amount of money available to service procurement officials in the early 1950s. Far too challenging a project to gain serious consideration today, Bu Aer

137634 is seen taxiing out into San Diego Bay. Employing a 60 degree sweep, thin-sectioned delta wing, the Seadart employed a retractable hydro-ski system reminiscent of the World War I Ursinus floatplane. This system was to create numerous problems with the handling of the aircraft on water over the 46 months of F2Y-1 flight testing and underwent several major modifications. A total of three Seadarts were built, the sole XF2Y-1 and two YF2Y-1 pre-production examples, one of which was lost, killing Convair's Charles E. Richbourg, during a Convair family day display on 4 November 1954. The crash cause was attributed to pilot induced oscillation. (Convair)

The **Convair XF2Y-1** is shown taxiing onto the beaching ramp. Note the small wheels at the rear of the machine's hydro-skis, supported by a centrally mounted retractable skid under the rear fuselage. Despite nearly four years and 300 flight hours of testing, re-engining from the original two 3,400lb s.t. Westinghouse J34-W-32s to 5,725lb s,t. Westinghouse J46s, plus much ongoing remedial work, the Seadart would have required a major Whitcombe-waisted re-design of its fuselage in order to achieve supersonic flight and was destined to remain in the 'development only' category. (Convair)

The rather ugly, corpulent appearance of the **S.F.E.C.M.A.S. 1405.02 Gerfaut II** belied the machine's impressive performance. Developed from the Gerfaut, first flown on 15 January 1954, the Gerfaut II's less than beauteous exterior was dictated by 'Area Ruling' a newly introduced means of minimising transonic drag rise. Devised by NACA aerodynamicist, Richard Whitcombe, 'Area Ruling' involved shaping the contours of an aircraft so that its overall cross-section rose and faded smoothly to zero along the machine's length. Also

known as 'waisting', as on the Grumman F11F-1 and Blackburn Buccaneer, 'Area Ruling' sometimes required bulges to be added. A halfway point along the line of Arsenal-devised wooden construction delta-winged gliders and Nord's impressive Griffon II, the Gerfaut was to become Europe's first aircraft to exceed Mach 1 without recourse to rocket boosting. Power for the Gerfaut was provided by a 6,170lb s.t. S.N.E.C.M.A. Atar 101C turbojet with reheat, the engine being mounted in one long air duct uninterrupted by cockpit and fuel tanks, etc., all of which are housed above, Aided by its area ruling, the Gerfaut could reach Mach 1.3 at 36,000 feet, or 859mph. (GIFAS)

Top The two **Republic XF-84H** jet-to-turboprop fighter conversions were developed by the US Air Force in the hope that a combination of turboprop engine and supersonic contra-rotating propeller would provide speeds comparable to the pure jet, but with greater fuel economy and thus an extension of the machine's radius of action. First flown on 22 July 1955 by Republic's Henry G. Beaird, the two XF-84Hs were converted to house the 5,850eshp Allison XT-40, developed for the US Navy. Ongoing engine and propeller-related problems killed the idea. Seen here is 51.17060, the second of the two XF-84HS. (US Air Force)

Almost universally known as 'Bea', **Wg. Cdr. Roland Beamont** is seen in this March 1973 photograph during final maker's testing of the Anglo-French single seat SEPCAT Jaguar GR 1. At this time, 'Bea' was Director of Flight Test for the British Aircraft

Corporation's Military Aircraft Division at Warton, Lancashire, the same place that he had joined in May 1947. 'Bea' had divided his war between fighter operations in Hawker Hurricanes, Typhoons and Tempests and fighter testing with Hawker. Joining English Electric as their Chief Test Pilot in 1947, Beamont went on to conduct the flight development of the Canberra, Lightning and BAC TSR-2 – English Electric having become a part of BAC at the start of 1960. 'Bea' is acknowledged as the first British pilot to exceed Mach 1 in level flight in a British aircraft, the English Electric P.1A in August 1954; and could make the same claim for Mach 2, following his 25 November 1958 flight in the Lightning F.1. (British Aircraft Corporation)

The **English Electric P.1A**, WG 760, progenitor of the Lightning, perhaps the one really outstanding British fighter of the thirty years following World War II. First flown on 4 August 1954, with 'Bea' Beamont at the controls, the twin 8,100lb s.t. unreheated Armstrong Siddeley Sapphire AS8a5-powered P.1A became the first British aircraft to exceed Mach 1 when it reached Mach 1.02 at 30,000 feet, or 692mph on 11 August just six days into flight testing. (English Electric)

Ugly, but innovative. The **Nord 1500.02 Griffon** prototype interceptor, seen here both at rest and in flight, employed a dual cycle propulsion system of turbojet mounted within a ramjet duct. The turbojet, in this case a 7,720lb s.t. S.N.E.C.M.A. Atar 101E, was necessary for take-off and initial acceleration into the ramjet's minimum speed for sustained ignition. From this point, the ramjet provided more and more of the impetus as the machine accelerated away in the climb. The Griffon, mainly in the hands of Andre Turcat, later to lead the French Concorde

flight test team, reached Mach 2.1 at 61,000 feet, at which time all of the incoming air was being diverted to the ramjet. Significantly, the Griffon, which made its maiden flight on 20 September 1955, continued to receive US Government research funding long after the US Congress had withdrawn funding support for other French research aircraft. Could it be that the Griffon, then routinely proving the validity of the dual-cycle engine during the latter half of the 1950, was also contributing technology for the upcoming mammoth Pratt & Whitney J58 dual-cycle engines used to power the Lockheed YF-12 and SR-71? (GIFAS)

Old prototypes never die, they usually 'soldier on' in some secondary role, as in this case of the prototype **Hawker Hunter F.6**, XF 833, seen here at the SBAC 1956 Farnborough Air Show, displaying its experimental thrust reverser system. Installed by Miles Aircraft earlier in the year, the system used two plates, normally lying flush with the fuselage sides, that could be swivelled into the jet's exhaust, deflecting it out and slightly forward to assist in stopping the aircraft. The idea worked.

Overleaf XD 145, the first of two **Saunders-Roe SR 53** mixed rocket- and jet-powered prototype interceptors that were to lead to the projected larger Saunders-Roe SR 177. The power for the SR 53 was provided by a 1,640lb s.t. Armstrong Siddeley Viper ASV8, fed by two small intakes just aft of the cockpit canopy, plus a hefty 8,000lb thrust DH Spectre rocket engine using High Test Peroxide in place of the more volatile liquid oxygen. XD 145's maiden flight took place on 16 May 1957 with the Company Chief Test Pilot at the controls, Sqn. Ldr. John Booth, who also took the second SR 53, XD 151 aloft just under seven months later, on 8 December. Capable of Mach 2 in level flight at 36,000 feet, SR 53 and SR 177 development was halted following the destruction of XD 151, on 5 June 1958.

According to the accident investigation, Booth, for reasons unknown, had decided to abort the take-off from Boscombe Down and had deployed the braking 'chute. Unfortunately, distance was not on Booth's side, the aircraft overshot the end of the runway, striking an approach lighting pole and exploded, killing Booth. (SARO Ltd)

The **Handley Page HP 115**, of which XP 841 was the only example, came about, like the BAC 221, as part of the flight test program associated with Concorde's development. Built to research the low speed handling of tender, or highly swept delta wings, the 1,900lb s.t. Bristol Siddeley Viper BSV9-powered machine first flew on 17 August 1961 at the RAE Bedford. With

its awesome 74.7 degrees of sweep back, the HP 115 looks as if it could bite back if mishandled, but to everyone's delight, it proved docile. The HP 115 continued giving yeoman service for many years until its retirement from flying at the start of 1974. (Handley Page)

Bristol's Type 188, first flown on 14 April 1962, could be truly considered a 'blast from the past' as its genesis was firmly rooted in the heady days of the early 1950s when Britain still entertained ambitions to produce a long-range bomber, capable of sustained supersonic cruise. One of the major contenders for this mantle was Avro 730, of which the Type 188 was a scaled-down aerodynamic and materials test vehicle. Issued to Bristol in February 1953, the contract to build two flight-worthy Type 188s, plus a static test airframe to Specification ER.134, resulted in a twin 14,000lb s.t. DH Gyron Junior DJR.1OR powered machine making much use of stainless steel to absorb the great heat generated by sustained flight at well above Mach 2. As it transpired, the Type 188 simply proved inadequate to the task, its highest level speed reached being Mach 1.88 at or above 36,000 feet, or 1,242mph and neither XF 923, or XF 926 could be persuaded to remain serviceable long enough to fly for any sustained period at over Mach 1. (Bristol)

The sole **Hunting H.126**, first flown on 26 March 1963, was built to investigate the 'Jet Flap' concept, developed by a team at Britain's National Gas Turbine Establishment. The idea was that by ducting the main bulk of jet engine exhaust to the wings, where it could flow out uniformly through a full span slot towards the wing's rear, this would aid wing lift and allow the use of a smaller, lighter wing. Powered by a 5,000lb s.t. Bristol Siddeley Orpheus 805, the H.126 seemed an overly complex means to prove the point, having a puffer jet, low speed control system and other such 'add-ons'. The H.126 made well over 100 flights, but there are indications that the amount of thermal insulation required by the exhaust distribution system

outweighed the intended structural weight savings. The other obvious question was what happened if the engine failed? (Hunting)

56.0756, the first of three **Lockheed NF-104As**, all modified during 1963 as part of the US Air Force-conducted Astronaut training programme operated from Edwards AFB. Using an additional 6,000lb thrust Rocketdyne AR-2 fitted on top of the rear fuselage, these machines were also fitted with a 'puffer jet' system to maintain attitude in the extremely thin air at and above 90,000 feet. A typical flight involved a steep zoom climb, arcing over into the horizontal somewhere between 90,000 and 100,000 feet. On 6 December 1963. Major R. W. Smith reached 118,860 feet, an unofficial record for aircraft taking off under their own power, as opposed to being air-launched. It was while flying one of these NF-104As that Col. Charles E. 'Chuck' Yeager nearly lost his life, when, following his ejection, his ejector seat charge set fire to his crash helmet. (US Air Force)

During the summer of 1959, the first of the two Fairey FD.2 high speed research deltas, WD 774, was singled out for major modification to help with the high speed phase of Concorde wing development. Transferred from the RAE, Bedford to BAC's Filton facility, WD 774 underwent major surgery, to emerge four and a half years later as the **BAC 221**, as seen here at its roll-out. First flown in this guise with its new ogival wing on 1 May 1964, this machine returned to RAE, Bedford in May 1966, from where it continued to fly for the next eight and a half years. (British Aircraft Corporation)

Faster, Higher, Further, 1946–1970

T his section is dedicated to those American scientists, designers, pilots and technicians who collectively took aviation by the scruff of the neck, instilled it with a sense of direction and purpose and, within the span of relatively few years turned 'aviation' into 'aerospace'. Mainly driven by the US Air Force and NACA through the medium of the manned 'X' plane series from X-1 to X-15, the Americans defined new parameters, not just in speed and altitude-setting records, but far more importantly, in pushing the subtler boundaries of a vast range of related activities adopted by commercial users as much as the military.

This was a truly fascinating period of aviation development; hindsight shows that it ended in a far more subdued atmosphere than it ought, with many questions still going unanswered. Why was this? A single political decision, causing a change of direction, was of paramount importance. When, in 1961, President John F. Kennedy launched America into the race for the moon, his action refocused much of the US's advanced aerospace research effort away from exploring manned flight into the hugely expensive arena of largely automated ballistic rocketry. Put simply, there were insufficient funds to meet the demands of the Gemini and Apollo ballistic programmes on top of existing research efforts. Kennedy's targeting the moon had set in concrete the shape of much of the US's advanced applied research for the major part of the 1960s.

Between 1946 and 1967, the US forged ahead with a well funded and generally well directed programme of research into all aspects of high speed flight. Despite occasional rivalries between the military and the civilian agencies, headed by NACA, latterly NASA, the effort remained focused and took the American aircraft to undreamed-of speeds and the very threshold of deep space. Typical of the early period of this endeavour was the US Navy's **Douglas D-558-II Skyrocket**, seen here being launched from its Boeing P2B-1S. This all-rocket powered machine, Bu Aer 37974, was the fastest of the trio of Skyrockets, reaching Mach 2.005 at 62,000 feet, or 1,291mph while diving back from its zenith at over 70,000 feet.

(Douglas Aircraft)

Below and right **Capt. Charles Elwood 'Chuck' Yeager** standing beside the **Bell XS-1** in which he was to carve his niche in the annals of aviation. 'Chuck' Yeager was born in mid-February 1923 in West Virginia. In the summer of 1941 Yeager enlisted in the US Army Air Corps as an aircraft mechanic. As in the case of many others, the nineteen-year-old Yeager's life would be transformed by the tides of war and, in the early months of 1942, he was selected for flying training. Gaining his 'wings' in June 1943, 'Chuck' joined the 3624th Fighter Squadron and got his first taste of combat flying North American P-51s out of Leiston, Suffolk, on 11 February 1944. Less than a month later, on 5 March, Yeager had his P-51 blown

away from around him by 20mm shells from a distinctly unfriendly FW 1-90 over France. Faced with capitulating to the occupying Germans, or attempting to evade them, Yeager opted for the latter and with the help of the French Resistance walked into neutral Spain before the month had ended. As a safeguard for the French Resistance, USAAF standing orders called for all evadees to be sent back to the US, but Yeager was not in a mind to go home quite yet and fought to remain in combat, pursuing his case all the way up to General Dwight D. Eisenhower in person. Commissioned in the summer of 1944, Yeager was to notch up 12 'kills', including five on one October day, prior to being posted back to the US in Mid-January 1945. This short but intensive personal war would have been enough for most by any measure, but not Yeager. Posted to Wright Field in July 1945 as a 22-year-old Captain in Flight Maintenance, Yeager grabbed the opportunity to fly anything and everything Wright, with its pick of new US and captured Axis types, had to offer. It was at this time that Yeager came to the notice of Col. Albert G. Boyd, Head of Flight Test, the man who was to bring Yeager into test flying and a career that was to see him leave the US Air Force in 1975 with the rank of Brigadier General. (US Air Force)

The two second generation **Bell X-1s** photographed at Edwards AFB Flight Test Centre. Overshadowed by their famous precursor, these two aircraft were to do so much in pushing outwards and upwards the boundaries of speed and altitude during the early half of the 1950s. Three of these X-1s had been built, the X-1A, the X-1B and the X-1D, the X-1C project never having materialised. By chance, the first of this trio to fly was the X-1D, on 24 July 1951, but its life was brief, ending just under a month later, on 22 August, when it was destroyed

following an in-flight explosion. Happily, its pilot, Lt. Col. Frank Everest had time to scramble back aboard the EB-50 prior to the X-1D's release. For its part, the X-1A, 48.1384, went on to reach a maximum speed of Mach 2.44, or 1,650mph on 12 December 1953 and climbed to 90,440 feet on 26 August 1954. Like the X-1D before it, the X-1A was ultimately to be jettisoned by its mother, on 8 August 1955, following a similar onboard explosion, the cause of which was eventually pinpointed, extraordinarily enough, as a chemical reaction between the liquid oxygen and Ulmer leather strapping used within the rocket fuel system. (Bell)

Below left During the early post-World War II years, the US Navy ran a parallel series of research aircraft to the US Air Force's X series. Somewhat more modest in aim and scale, these Navy machines, led by the Douglas Skystreak and Skyrocket, nonetheless added materially to the sum of data obtained. First flown on 27 May 1947, three **Douglas D558-1 Skystreaks** were built to explore aircraft handling in the trans-sonic speed range. Powered by a 5,000lb s.t. Allison J35-A-11, the Skystreak proved to be a stalwart research tool, but, as happened all too frequently in these early days of the jet, the second aircraft Bu Aer 37.971, was to be lost, on 3 May 1948, when its engine compressor broke up, destroying the aircraft and killing NACA test pilot, Howard Lilly. (Douglas Aircraft)

Overleaf **Edward Henry 'Ed' Heinemann** inspecting the wing leading edge slots of the first Douglas D-558-11 Skyrocket. After joining the Douglas Aircraft Company in 1926, Heinemann's talents as a designer soon brought him to the forefront. Seconded to the newly formed, part Douglas owned Northrop Corporation at El Segundo in 1932, Heinemann lead the design of the Northrop BT-I, precursor to the famed Douglas SBD Dauntless. Staying at El Segundo, which in September 1937 reverted back to Douglas, Heinemann went on to lead the design of all Douglas's non-transport types for the US Navy, from the SBD Dauntless, through the Skystreak

and Skyrocket, to the superb A-4 Skyhawk. Heinemann's sure touch was also behind the company's A-20 Havoc and its equally illustrious successor the A-26, later B-26 invader. Retiring from Douglas with the closure of their El Segundo Division, Heinemann continued as a design consultant. After what he had achieved with the A-4 Skyhawk in terms of re-introducing 'the small is beautiful' concept to aircraft design, it was perhaps inevitable that General Dynamics would hire his consultative services for their compact, low-cost F-16 fighter, a machine Heinemann played no small part in defining. (Douglas Aircraft)

Centre, below Designed during the last four months of 1945, the mixed rocket- and turbojet-powered **Douglas D-558-II Skyrocket** was drawn up to meet a US Navy requirement for a supersonic successor to the Skystreak, capable of taking off and landing under its own power. Seen here in its original form still at El Segundo, is the first D-558-11, Bu Aer 37973, prior to being trucked to Muroc Dry Lake on 10 December 1947. First flown on 4 February 1948, pilot criticism led to modifications, including a new, raised cockpit canopy, along with a taller fin to improve directional stability. Incidentally, the first flight was made on the power of the machine's 3,000lb s.t. Westinghouse J34-W-40, as the 6,000lb thrust Reaction Motors XLR-8-RM-5 was yet to become available. (Douglas Aircraft)

Centre, above The first of the **Douglas Skyrocket** trio, seen here in later form with rocket engine firing. Note the forward, low mounted jet engine intakes and its exhaust outlet, the dark area just under the national marking on the fuselage. This first machine underwent many modifications, ultimately having its turbojet completely removed to make way for extra rocket fuel, which forced it to be air-launched, the second D-558-11 was similarly stripped of its jet for the same purpose. As previously metnioned, the second Skyrocket, Bu Aer 37974, later NACA 144, can lay claim to being the first aircraft to exceed Mach 2, when in the hands of NACA's Scott Crossfield, on 20 November 1953, it reached Mach 2.005 at 62,000 feet, or 1,291mph in a dive from 72,000 feet. (Douglas Aircraft)

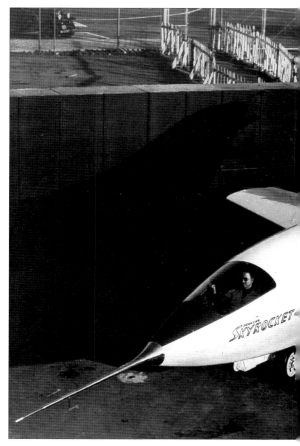

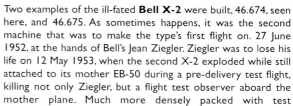

Two examples of the ill-fated **Bell X-2** were built, 46.674, seen here, and 46.675. As sometimes happens, it was the second machine that was to make the type's first flight on. 27 June 1952, at the hands of Bell's Jean Ziegler. Ziegler was to lose his life on 12 May 1953, when the second X-2 exploded while still attached to its mother EB-50 during a pre-delivery test flight, killing not only Ziegler, but a flight test observer aboard the mother plane. Much more densely packed with test

instrumentation than any of its predecessors, the sole remaining X-2 was delivered to Edwards AFB in time for Capt. Frank Everest to make its first gliding release from the EB-50A on 10 October 1953. From this point on, Everest, (above) conducted most of the X-2 flying. The X-2's last flight was to be made on 27 September 1962, with Capt. Milburn Apt at the controls – his first flight in the X-2. After reaching Mach 3.196, or 2,094mph, on its descent through 66,000 feet, the machine commenced to topple around most of its axes as a result of roll-coupling effects. Apt used the aircraft's escape capsule at 40,000 feet, but apparently then left it too late to extricate himself from the capsule and parachute to safety. Ironically, the X-2 having made a leaf-like descent to earth, had suffered minimum damage on impact. (US Air Force, via Bell)

Overleaf **Douglas's** sole **X-3**, built for the US Air Force and serialled 4.9.2892. An unmitigated disaster, this 'flying fuselage', with its minuscule wings made its first tentative hop into the

air on 15 October 1952, with its official first flight occurring five days later, on the 20th. From this point onwards, everything about the X-3 appears to have gone downhill with a vengeance. Grossly underpowered by its two 4,850lb s.t. reheated Westinghouse J34-WE-175, the highly wing loaded X-3 initially showed a great reluctance to fly at all, with a lift-off speed of 260mph! Once airborne, the X-3, far from being able to explore flight behaviour at around Mach 2 could only achieve Mach 0.95 at 31,000 feet, or 641mph. On one occasion the X-3 reached Mach 1.21, but this was in a 30-degree dive under full power and with the machine displaying some fairly frightening handling habits. In all, the X-3 made 51 flights, ending in May 1956. While the physical size limitations of the airframe prevented the use of other, more powerful engines, the unloved X-3 did make one contribution to aviation progress, in that its wing was to provide the aerodynamic form for that adopted by Lockheed's Clarence 'Kelly' Johnson in designing the F-104 Starfighter. (Douglas Aircraft)

The **Leduc 021.01** was the last of a series of relatively low speed ramjet demonstrators developed by Rene Leduc, who had pioneered the ramjet development. Like its forebears, the 021 needed to be launched from the modified Sud Est SE 161 Lanquedoc mother ship. Design limited to Mach 0.85 at 35,000 feet, or 562mph, the 021's integral ramjet provided a formidable 13,200lb of thrust at this speed and altitude. To get home, the 021, of which two were built, housed a 836lb s.t. Turbomeca Mabore 11 within the ramjet duct. The 021's first powered flight was made on 7 August 1953, following upon which both 021s were tested at altitudes between 33,000 and 66,000 feet, contributing to the development of the Nord 1500 Griffon. (GIFAS)

Below The former NACA test pilot Scott Crossfield goes through the strapping-in process as the first **X-15** hangs from its pylon beneath its Boeing B-52 mother ship preparatory to its first captive flight on 10 March 1959. Crossfield went on to make the first unpowered flight three months later, on 8 June, and flew it another seven times prior to its hand-over to NASA in early 1960. By this time, Crossfield had flown the machine to Mach 2.53, or 1,669mph, and had demonstrated a 6 'g' manoeuvring ability. (North American)

Above The first of the three **North American X-15s**, 56.6670, with its initial and interim, twin barrel Reaction Motors XLRII engine, awaits disassembly for trucking to Edwards AFB. The aircraft's tail section is resting on a ground handling trolley. in place of the twin ventral skids normally deployed for landing. Ultimately, the X-15 would take its pilots into totally new areas of flight by exceeding Mach 6 and to altitudes beyond any effective atmosphere. (North American)

Right Full frontal on the second of the **X-15** trio, 56.6671, after being re-built and fitted with these two, huge external fuel tanks to feed its fuel hungry, fully throttlable, 50,000lbb thrust, single-chamber Reaction Motors XLR99, the definitive propulsion for all three aircraft. The second X-15 was to fly fastest, reaching Mach 6.7, or 4,534mph and the highest, climbing to 354,200 feet, or just over 67 miles up. In all, the trio of X-15s amassed a total of 199 flights, with one fatality, that of Major Michael Adams, while flying the third X-15 when it broke up at Mach 3.57 or 3,856mph and 125,000 feet, on 15 November 1967. The cause of the severe pitching forces that exceeded the aircraft's design limits was attributed in part to a one-off self-adaptive flight control system being trialled on this X-15. (North American)

Overleaf **Boeing's** promising **X-20 Dyna-Soar**, seen here in an artist's impression of it shedding its cockpit re-entry heat shield preparatory to landing. This single seat orbital aerospace

plane provided its pilot with a large measure of manoeuvrability, or cross-range capability, allowing him to select his landing site from over a broad radius, unlike the Gemini and Apollo capsules, whose watery splash-down sites were extremely predictable. In operation, the X-20 would have been a physically small element in a much larger system, with the Dyna-Soar sitting atop and spearheading a Martin Titan III intercontinental ballistic missile, modified to serve as a launch/boost vehicle.designed to be capable of placing the X-20 into low orbit at around Mach 25, or approximately 18,000mph. The first X-20, with its own 16,000lb rocket engine for orbital manoeuvring, was in assembly and was scheduled to make its first orbital flight in mid-1965 when cancelled. (Boeing)

Right The chosen few. The six selected to fly **Boeing's X-20**, five US Air Force pilots and NASA's Milton O. Thompson stand beside a full-size mock-up of the machine, seen here in its final form, complete with 16,000lb thrust manoeuvring rocket engine at the rear. Cancelled on 15 December 1963, after six years of development effort and the expenditure of around $500 million, the X-20 was to fall victim to the Apollo manned ballistic system. that was to cost in excess of $24 billion in the coming years. (Boeing)

Opposite, above The **NASA-Northrop M2-F2**, first flown unpowered by NASA's chief lifting body research pilot, Milton O. Thompson on 12 July 1966, Northrop's own briefing on the flight is worth quoting. 'The flight required 4 minutes from its 45,000 feet launch (from a Boeing B-52) to touchdown. The initial glide was very steep, with a 250 feet per second sink rate (or 170.5mph vertically) before the vehicle is 'flared' to decrease the sink rate to a more comfortable 5 to 10 feet per second at 1,200 feet above the ground. (Most pilots would be

appy with 5 feet per second.) During the 'flare', indicated air peed falls from 350mph to 250mph and as low as 190mph at ouchdown'. The hazards of such landing speeds could be /itnessed at the start of each episode of the television series The Six Million Dollar Man', which shows what happened hen NASA pilot Bruce A. Peterson lost control of the M2-F2 May 1967. (Northrop)

The sole **Martin Marietta X-24A** lifting body, 66.13551, was the last of this peculiar breed and perhaps the most advanced. Unlike the two NASA lifting bodies, the X-24A used a lenticular shape and was the fruit of a collaborative effort by the US Air Force's Flight Development Laboratory and Martin Marietta. As with the rest of this clan, the X-24A's purpose was

to explore the best shape for an orbital aerospace 'plane and its post re-entry handling. Air-launched like its NASA soul mates, the X-24 made its first unpowered flight on 17 April 1969, followed, on 19 March 1970, by its first under the impetus of its 8,480lb thrust Thiokol XLR-RM-13. Typically, a 2.5 minute powered climb to 70,000 feet and Mach 1.6 would be followed by a five minute descent to landing. (Martin Marietta)

Left and below **NASA-Northrop's HL-10** lifting body about to touch down at Edwards AFB at the end of its unpowered maiden flight on 22 December 1966. Northrop developed two quite separate series of lifting body research aircraft during the 1960s, the M2 family for NASA's Ames Research Centre on the west coast, along with the HL-10 for NASA's Virginia-based Langley Research Centre. While all internal systems were identical, the aircraft's external shapes differed: the HL-10 resembled a very thick airfoil, while the M2 was shaped like a half cone, the flat side facing upwards. Both were air-launched from a Boeing B-52 and both were powered by an 8,000lb thrust Thiokol XLRII rocket engine. A typical HL-10 flight consisted of a powered climb from the launch altitude of 45,000 feet to 85,000 feet and Mach 1.9 in 100 seconds, followed by a steep 3 to 4 minute descent into a 180-190mph touchdown. As summarised by NASA HL-10 Project Pilot, Bruce A. Peterson, 'it was like landing at the end of a 30 degree dive bombing run.' Below is a view of the HL-10 suspended under the Boeing B-52 launch aircraft. (Northrop)

Vertical Flight without Rotors, 1954–1967

As far back as the early 1930s Charles H. Zimmerman, with his 'Propwash Emersed Wing' concept, was getting close to the idea of VTOL, Vertical Take-Off and Landing. The big impetus, however, came with World War II and the new generation of powerful piston, jet and even rocket engines, all of which promised the would-be VTOL designers that one thing they needed more than anything – a greater power-to-weight ratio. German designers were the most fertile of thinkers at this time, not only did they come up with the vertically-launched, rocket powered Bachem Ba 349A Natter, Focke-Wulf and Focke-Achgelis came up with VTOL projects in the shape of ramjet powered rotor-cum-wing interceptor and a tilt-propellered utility type, respectively.

Interest in VTOL appeared to fade in the years immediately following World War II, except perhaps in the US, where the US Navy sought the elusive VTOL 'quarter-deck' fighter, while the US Army envisaged the individual 'flying infantryman', each standing on his own ducted fan. By the early 1950s, American affluence was ensuring a seemingly inexhaustible supply of weird and wonderful VTOL solutions, these were not just paper designs either, for the most part they were flyable prototypes.

By the late 1950s, all this American effort began to take shape as the armed services started to take VTOL more seriously. Foreshadowing the Bell-Boeing V-22 Osprey of today, things started to crystallise around the turboprop-powered tilt-wing machine. In Europe, the British, French and Germans were starting to look at jet-powered VTOL. Why the US and Europe differed in their views about the ideal type of power to employ reflected the state of their respective aero-engine industries. Since World War II, European engine makers had tended to concentrate on jets at the expense of turboprops, whereas a number of major US engine producers could all offer high-powered turboprops virtually off-the-shelf.

By the 1960s, most of the significant VTOL thinking both in the US and Europe was coming to fruition. The US was driving rapidly towards producing a tri-service VTOL assault transport in the shape of the LTV-Hiller-Ryan XC-142A, while Britain and France were contesting the lighter, faster end of the potential VTOL market with their P.1127 Kestrel and Dassault's Balzac/Mirage 111-V demonstrators. Overall, the picture wasn't quite so clear cut. For instance, the Americans may have been spending most of their VTOL cash on the 'heavies', but they still had enough spare to enable them to fund the major share of the first multi-national P.1127 Kestrel squadron to be formed at RAF West Raynham in late 1964. German industry was working away on a multitude of VTOL designs, ranging from single seat interceptor and strike types to the large Dornier Do.31 jet-powered transport. By the end of the 1960s many of the more grandiose VTOL plans and aspirations lay in tatters, the US had dropped the XC-142, a similar fate had befallen the Do.31, leaving the Hawker Harrier as the only credible looking survivor.

The 1960 prototype **Hawker P.1127**, sire to the now extended, international family of Harrier variants.

Above The sole, company-funded **Bell Model 65 Air Test Vehicle**, or ATV, N 1105V, may have been a modest, unbeautiful machine, but it was the first in the world to rise and descend on jet power alone. It can also claim to be the first aircraft to flight test an air reaction, or 'puffer jet' secondary flight control system, needed to maintain aircraft attitude when operating at speed below which the normal controls can function. N 1105V, built from parts of other light aircraft was powered by two 1,110lb s.t. Fairchild J44-R-1s, while a Turbomeca Palouste provided compressed air for the puffer jets. Bell's ATV first hovered freely in January 1954, subsequently amassing four and a half hours aloft. (Bell)

Opposite The tail-sitting **Lockheed XFV-1** was designed not as a research machine, but to full pre-production fighter standards. It was required to demonstrate the ability to operate on and off small platforms readily fitted to either warships or merchant vessels. Powered by the same 5,500eshp Allison XT40-A-6 as installed on the rival XFY-1, Lockheed's XFV-1 first flew on 16 June 1954, a month and a half before the XFY-1. However, this flight involved a completely conventional, rolling take-off, made with the machine straddling an ungainly fixed landing gear resembling a Zimmer frame. Although emerging ahead of its rival, Lockheed XFV-1 Bu Aer 138657 never managed to make a vertical ascent from a standing start, any transition from the horizontal to the vertical was made at a safe altitude. A fact that even the most creative of Lockheed publicists would find difficult to hide from the Navy. (Lockheed)

Below The British had been flying the visually attention-grabbing 'Deflected Thrust' Gloster Meteor flight test bed for some years, but even with this priming, there were few ready to accept **Rolls-Royce's Thrust Measuring Rig**, or TMR, as anything less than an aeronautical aberration. How wrong they were was soon to be proved, for while never coming close to such 'tail sitters' as the XFV-1 and XFY-1, or Ryan X-13 in relation to aircraft structural norms, the curious TMR, with its two 5,000lb s.t. Rolls-Royce Nenes mounted back-to-back and its puffer jet stabilisation led directly to Europe's first 'flat riser', Short's SC.I, while the 'tail sitters' led nowhere. Dubbed the 'Flying Bedstead' by the press, the TMR made its first

untethered flight on 3 August 1954, in the capable hands of Capt. R. T. Shepperd and marginally under a year after its first tethered outing. two TMRs were built and allocated serial nos XJ 314 and XK 426. The fact that testing these cumbersome devices, capable of little more than 34mph horizontally, or going above 50 feet, was still dangerous was to be horribly illustrated when the second TMR struck the gantry to which it was tethered and crashed, killing its RAF pilot, Wg. Cdr. H. G. F. Larson. (Rolls-Royce)

The fruit of US Navy studies into convoy protection carried out between 1947 and 1950, the **Convair XFY-1** and its Lockheed rival were both ordered in March 1951. Like its XFV-1 counterpart, the Convair used the massive 5,500 eshp Allison XT40-A-6 and was built to the same exacting pre-production fighter standards. While the Convair machine did not make its first flight until 1 August 1954, Convair's Project Pilot, James F. 'Skeets' Coleman, did ultimately manage a number of transitional flights made from a standing start. The fact that flying this 'tail sitter' straight up off the ground and back down, while virtually reclining on your back with little outside visible cueing, called for a certain degree of intestinal fortitude was confirmed by the award of the coveted Harmon

Trophy to 'Skeets' Coleman in 1956. The sole XFY-1 Bu Aer 138648 had an estimated top level speed of 610mph at 15,000 feet. (Convair)

Taken over by the US Air Force from an original US Navy programme, **Ryan's X-13 Vertijet** 'tail sitter' weighed 7,313lb and had a 10.000lb s.t. Rolls-Royce Avon RA-28-49 engine. Given this excess of power-to-weight there was no doubting that the X-13 could rise vertically off the ground, or, for that matter, sink back to earth or sea in a controlled manner: the problem was how to achieve these terminal flight stage feats while operating off small shipboard platforms, which is what the X-13 had been all about until the winter of 1953-1954, when the cash-strapped Navy was forced to withdraw further funding. The method developed by Ryan was ingenious and involved a transporter-cum-launch/landing platform. In the former role, the X-13 was transported horizontally, prior to being hydraulically jacked, along with its platform, into the vertical, from where it climbed away. For retrieval, the X-13's pilot needed to vertically lower the machine close enough to the platform to be able to engage a 'sky-hook' system, initiated by a glorified fishing line, that drew the aircraft into the platform's securing grapples. First flown conventionally on 10 December 1955, the first vertical lift-off followed on 28 May 1956. Two X-13s were built and both survived numerous full transitional flights to retire to museums. (Ryan)

With a flight test career spanning more than twenty four years, **Bell's** sole **Model 68 X-14A** proved to be a particularly useful, if largely unsung, research tool. Serialled 56.4022, the X-14 started its free hovering life on 17 February 1957. At this time the machine was powered by two 1,560lb s.t. Armstrong Siddeley Viper ASs, later being re-engined to take two 2,850lb SA General Electric J85-GE-5s, at which time it became the X-14A. Carrying on from where the Bell ATV left off, the X-14 employed vectored thrust to deflect the main engine exhaust downwards during jetborne flight, with main engine bled air being supplied to operate the puffer controls for attitude stabilisation. The X-14 was the first aircraft ever to use vectored thrust to achieve vertical flight. The X-14A, which reached 174mph, carried on flying until 29 May 1981, when it was damaged by fire following a hard landing. (Bell)

A particularly fitting photograph of **Thomas W. 'Tom' Brooke-Smith** with the Short SC.1 as backdrop. As Shorts' Chief Test Pilot, Tom Brooke-Smith had nurtured this 'flat riser' with some potentially lethal handling aspects from inception through and beyond completion of the makers' testing phase. Indeed, it was during a later delivery flight that he was to bring the aircraft safely to rest, following the simultaneous bursting of several tyres at around 178mph during a conventional take-off. 'Tom' Brooke-Smith was one of the few who came to test flying via a non-military route, by gaining a pre-World War II civilian pilot's licence and wartime ferry flying with Britain's Air Transport Auxiliary. Overleaf is **Shorts' SC.1**, of which two were built in the 1955 to 1956 period, developed to study the low speed end of a British research programme into VTOL. The basic propulsive layout adopted by Shorts can be seen in the ground view of the ill-fated second machine, XG 905. It consisted of a single, rear-mounted 2,130lb s.t. Rolls-Royce RB 108 for forward flight and four more RB 108s mounted vertically in the central fuselage to provide vertical lift. As was fast becoming the practice, puffer jets were used for attitude control while operating at low speed or in the hover. First flown conventionally on 2 April 1957, XG 905 hovered for the first

time just over a year later, on 28 May 1958, which in turn led to the first full transitional flight on 6 April 1960. Sadly, XG 905 was to crash on 2 October 1963, fatally injuring its RAE test pilot, J. R. Green. On the right is a view from beneath showing the underside of the four vertically mounted RB 108 lift jets. (Shorts)

The one-off **Hiller X-18**, 57.3078, was built to prove the applicability of tilt wing technology to future large VTOL transport aircraft. Powered by two 55,850eshp Allison XT40-A-14 turboprops, the X-18 first flew on 20 November 1959. As seen here, the X-18 is flying with 20 degrees of wing tilt, readily verified by the prominent test marks. Although the X-18's wing could be tilted to a maximum of 90 degrees, the machine was never flown with more than 35 degree of tilt, ensuring that all take-off and landings be made in the conventional manner. Flight testing of the X-18 was looking very promising up until its twentieth flight in July 1961. During this flight, with the wing at a 25 degrees tilt, one of the powerful turboprop propellers' pitch control failed, causing the aircraft to promptly roll onto its back. This all occurred at 10,000 feet, from where the inverted X-18 commenced to spin down. The two test pilots aboard chose to stay and managed to recover from the inverted spin at very low altitude. The X-18 never flew again. (US Air Force)

Overleaf An 'in Country' photograph of 62.5925, the last of the five **LTV-Hiller-Ryan XC-142As** built, showing its ability to operate in and out of a desert strip during May 1965 trials in the Mojave area. The XC-142A was powered by four 3,080eshp General Electric T64-GE-1 turboprops. The XC-142A spurned the puffer jet control of the Hiller X-18 in favour of using the differential propeller thrust management approach, the one problem with this was that it required the small, tail-mounted

propeller, just visible under the slab tailplane, to maintain pitch axis control. It was the failure of this propeller that led to the one flight test fatal crash on 10 May 1967, killing the three LTV pilots, Stuart G, Madison., John Ornvig and Charles Jester. Capable of accommodating two pilots and 32 fully equipped troops, the XC-142A's top level speed was 431mph at 20,000 feet, at which height it cruised at 253mph. The machine's tactical radius of action with full load ranged from 230 to 470 miles, depending on whether the departure and arrival were vertical or conventional. First flown from a rolling take-off on 26 September 1964, the first hover took place late in December, followed by the first full transitional flight on 11 January 1965. The five XC-142As amassed 420 flying hours during 488 flights, the aircraft being handled by no less than 39 military and civilian pilots during the 1964 to 1967 period. Arguably, the XC-142A came very close to providing the world with its first effective VTOL transport. The aircraft had problems, but its biggest was undoubtedly its timing: its arrival coincided with the height of American involvement in South East Asia and the military clearly had more pressing calls upon its allotted funds. (LTV)

Right XP 831, the first of two prototype **Hawker P.1127s**, formates on XP 972, the first of four Hawker P.1127 Kestrel pre-production development types. XP 831 had started life as a purely company-funded venture, only being contracted by the Ministry of Supply in September 1960. Initial tethered testing of XP 831 commenced in October and on 19 November 1960, the machine made its first free hovering flight with Hawker's Chief Test Pilot, Sqn. Ldr. A. W. 'Bill' Bedford at the controls. Power for the aircraft came from a Bristol Pegasus vectored thrust turbofan, the rated output of which climbed from an initial 10.500lb s.t. to 13.500 lb s.t. over the twenty-month flying life of XP 831.prior to its June 1962 very public mishap at the Paris Air Show. Despite the extensive damage to the aircraft,

Bill Bedford's injuries were slight. XP 9972's career was even shorter lived, when, following its 5 April 1962 first flight, it was irreparably damaged on 30 October 1962 during a forced landing resulting from engine failure and an in-flight fire. Despite these early setbacks, the Hawker's P.1127 and Kestrel evolved into the Harrier, still the West's only series-produced VTOL combat aircraft. (Hawker)

Above The West German **EWP Sud's VJ101C X-1**, the first of two prototypes for a projected Mach 2 VTOL interceptor bore a strong resemblance to the earlier Bell D-188A project designed to meet the same mission. However, according to Bell, despite numerous similarities, the two designs were not related. The fruit of an industrial collaboration between Heinkel, Bolkow and Messerschmitt, plus much government cash, the VJ101Cs used six 2,750lb s.t. Rolls-Royce RB 145 turbojets, arranged in pairs, with two each in swivelling pods at the wingtips, plus two in the forward fuselage, just aft of the cockpit. During jetborne or hovering flight, this triangulation of thrust could be either manually or automatically fine-tuned to provide altitude control, obviating the need for a puffer jet system. In forward flight, the two fuselage engines would shut down, all propulsion coming from the now horizontal wingtip pods. The X-1 first hovered on 10 April 1963, making its first full transitional flight on 20 September 1963. Unfortunately, it was to crash and be destroyed in the autumn of the following year. While the X-1 had always been destined to be the low speed vehicle, the X-2, by virtue of carrying 3,550lb s.t. reheated RB 145 in the wingtip pods was to be used for testing at speeds up to Mach 1.08. The X-2 first flew on 12 June 1965, followed by its first full transition on 22 October 1965. Soon afterwards, the programme for the projected VJ101D production aircraft was cancelled which made the remaining prototype redundant. (EWP Sud)

Overleaf The **Dassault Balzac** was a low speed VTOL demonstrator conversion of the first Dassault Mirage III airframe. Using the same basic separate lift, cruise and puffer jet arrangement proven on the Short SC.1, the Balzac's forward propulsion was furnished by a 5,000lb s.t. Bristol Siddeley Orpheus, while the lifting power came from eight 2,200lb s.t. Rolls-Royce RB 108s that shut down once the machine had transitioned to forward flight. Used as a test bed for the larger Mirage 111-V VTOL fighter prototype the Balzac made its first untethered flight on 18 October 1963, just over three months later, on 24 January 1964, the Balzac crashed, killing its pilot. It was rebuilt and again crashed on 5 September 1965, tragically killing another pilot. By this time, it seemed that what interest there was in VTOL combat aircraft was focusing on the Harrier with its vectored thrust engine, for which the go-ahead had been given in early 1965. Dassault quietly dropped

development of their VTOL proposals, defeated by the need to carry the extra weight of ,and fuel for, the lift engines that for the major part of each flight were simply dead weight. (Dassault)

Below **Yakovlev's Yak-36**, NATO code-name 'Freehand', was developed during the early 1960s and first revealed to the public in July 1967. Around Twelve of these VTOL research machines are believed to have been built and clearly played a major part in the development of the operational, seagoing Yakovlev Yak-36MP 'Forger' VTOL strike fighter first flown during 1971 and initially deployed aboard the Soviet *Moskva* class through deck cruisers in mid-1976. Although the research aircraft carried two, large vectored thrust engines in the same fuselage flanking position as the later production aircraft, they appeared to lack the two quite separate lift-only engines that are carried in the forward fuselage of the carrier strike fighter.

Opposite, above The first of **Bell Aerosystems's** curious looking **X-22As**, Bu Weap 151520, was first flown on 17 March 1966, but was damaged beyond repair just under five months later on 8 August. However, by now the second X-22A, BU Weap 151521 was ready to take up the task of flight testing the tandem, tilt ducted fan concept, continuing its flying well into the mid-1980s. Four 1,250eshp General Electric YTS8-GE-BD turboshaft engines powered the X-22As, giving the machines a maximum speed of 255mph and a range of 445 miles, However, far more important than its speed was the X-22A's ability not Just to carry its two man crew aloft, but to provide for the carriage of up to 1,200lb of flight test equipment within its spacious box-sectioned fuselage. (Bell Aerosystems)

Below right **Nord's 500** represented the minimalist route to tilt ducted fan research, employing two 317shp Allison T63-A-5A

turboshafts. Similar in concept to two earlier American machines, the Doak 16 and Bell Aerosystems X-22A, the Nord 500 went one stage further by embodying a shutter system at the rear of its ducted fans in an endeavour to enhance hover performance by controlling airflow expansion. Two Nord 550s were built, the first in early 1967, followed in 1968 by the second, seen here undergoing tethered tests on 23 July 1968 with Armand Jacquet at the controls. Overall stability problems may have led to the abandonment of this programme. (GIFAS)

Right Europe's answer to the US turboprop-powered LTV-Hiller-Ryan XC-142A was the Jet-powered **Dornier Do.31E3**. First flown on 14 July 1967, using a rolling take-off, the Do.31 made its first hover on 22 November 1967, followed by its first transitions during mid-December 1967. Power for

the Do.31 in vertical flight was provided by the combination of its eight 4,400lb s.t. Rolls-Royce RB 162-4D wingtip-mounted lift Jets and its two 15,500lb s.t. Bristol Pegasus 5-2 vectored thrust turbofans. Once aloft, forward flight of up to a top level speed of 400mph at 19,685 feet was achieved on the output of the two Pegasus turbofans alone. Capable of carrying 16 fully equipped troops, flight testing of the Do.31 continued into 1970 and the machine was considered sufficiently reliable to be flight demonstrated at the Paris Air Show. The Do.31 programme was brought to a close in April 1970 with the withdrawal of further government funding. Impressive as the Dornier Do.31 was, it seems that the cost of achieving verticality sacrificed too much in terms of payload/range capability, not to mention the astronomic initial, and ongoing maintenance costs associated with such a complex machine. (Dornier)

Index